P9-AFY-966

SPELLING WORKOUT

Phillip K. Trocki

Modern Curriculum Press
Parsippany

EXECUTIVE EDITOR   Wendy Whitnah

PROJECT EDITOR   Diane Dzamtovski

EDITORIAL DEVELOPMENT
DESIGN AND PRODUCTION   The Hampton-Brown Company

ILLUSTRATORS   Anthony Accardo, Joe Boddy, Roberta Collier-Morales, Mark Farina,
Sandra Forrest, Carlos Freire, Meryl Henderson, Jane McCreary,
Masami Miyamoto, Deborah Morse, Rik Olson, Doug Roy, John Sandford,
Rosalind Solomon.

PHOTO CREDITS   5, Boyd Norton/Comstock; 6, Uniphoto/Pictor; 9, Uniphoto/Pictor;
17, Prenzel/Animals Animals; 29, Curt Anderson/Courtesy of Schmitt Music Co.;
33, Nancy Brown/Image Bank; 41, Lynn M. Stone/Image Bank;
43, David de Lossy/Image Bank; 45, Andy Caulfield/Image Bank;
50, Lawrence Migdale; 61, Michael S. Thompson/Comstock; 64, Photo Researchers;
65, Archive Photos; 69, David Ryan/Uniphoto; 72, Comstock;
77, Michael P. Gadomski/Photo Researchers; 85, Mary Kate Denny/Photo Edit;
101, Michael Skott/Image Bank; 103, Grant Huntington;
105, Deborah Gilbert/Image Bank; 113, Todd Eberle;
116, Michael S. Thompson/Comstock; 129, Chris Alan Wilton/Image Bank;
133, Rafael Macia/Photo Researchers; 136, Paul Shambroom/Photo Researchers;
137, Boyd Norton/Comstock.

COVER DESIGN   The Hampton-Brown Company
COVER PHOTO   Romilly Lockyer/Image Bank

Typefaces for the manuscript and cursive type in this book were provided
by Zaner-Bloser, Inc., Columbus, Ohio, copyright, 1993.

Copyright © 1994 by Modern Curriculum Press, Inc.

MODERN CURRICULUM PRESS
299 Jefferson Road, Parsippany, NJ 07054

ISBN 0-8136-2817-2

3 4 5 6 7 8 9 10 PO OO 99 98 97

TABLE OF CONTENTS

Learning to Spell a Word

1. Say the word.
   Look at the word and say the letters.

2. Print the word with your finger.

3. Close your eyes and think of the word.

4. Cover the word and print it on paper.

5. Check your spelling.

Making a Spelling Notebook

A Spelling Notebook will help you when you write. Write the words you're having trouble with on a sheet of paper. Add the paper to a notebook or folder. Whenever you need help to spell a word, look in your Spelling Notebook.

Name _____

Consonants

Warm Up

What is almost nine feet tall and lays eggs?

A Big Bird!

What has feathers, runs **fast**, and is taller than the tallest basketball player? It's the biggest **bird** in the world, the ostrich. This giant bird can grow to be almost **nine** feet tall. The largest ones live in North Africa. Some people think that ostriches bury their heads in the sand. They say that the ostriches are hiding from their enemies.

Just think about these facts. An ostrich can weigh as much as 350 pounds. One kick from an ostrich foot can **kill** a **person**. As you can see, the ostrich has no reason to hide from anything. It can run faster than its enemies anyway. The ostrich does have one problem. It **cannot** fly!

Ostrich hens lay their eggs in holes in the sand. One **egg** is often larger than a softball. The shell of the egg is very strong. It won't break even if a person stands on it. If you wanted to hard-boil one egg, you'd need plenty of **water**. When it was done, you could use it to make as much egg salad as two dozen chicken eggs would make. That's **quite** a meal!

Say the words in dark print in the selection. What consonant sounds do you hear?

On Your Mark

Take your Warm Up Test. Then check your spelling with the List Words on the next page.

The alphabet has two kinds of letters. The **vowels** are **a, e, i, o, u,** and sometimes **y** and **w.** All the other letters are **consonants.** Read the List Words. Some words have more than one syllable, as in <u>forest</u>. Notice that each syllable has its own vowel sound.

LIST WORDS

1. fast *fast* ✓
2. bird *bird*
3. nine *nine*
4. life *life*
5. since *since*
6. kill *kill*
7. cannot *cannot*
8. egg *egg*
9. water *water*
10. mark *mark*
11. person *person*
12. quite *quite*
13. beside *beside*
14. sister *sister*
15. forest *forest*

Game Plan

✱ Spelling Lineup

Write the List Words that have one syllable.

1. _fast_
2. _bird_
3. _nine_
4. _life_
5. _kill_
6. _egg_
7. _mark_
8. _qutite_
9. _since_

✱ Write the List Words that have two syllables.

10. _forest_
11. _cannot_
12. _water_
13. _person_
14. _beside_
15. _sister_

Missing Letters

Write letters to finish the List Words in the sentences. Then write the List Words.

1. The ostrich is a large b i r d .   bird

2. Some ostriches are N i N e feet tall.   Nine

3. That's taller than a very tall p e r s o n .   person

4. An ostrich e g g weighs about three pounds!   egg

5. An ostrich can k i l l an enemy with one kick. kill

Word Parts

A compound word is a word made by joining two or more words. Find the compound word in each sentence. Circle the part of the compound word that spells a List Word. Then write the List Word.

1. Break(fast) is a morning meal.   fast

2. A (life)guard keeps swimmers safe.   life

3. A book(mark) keeps my place in a book.   mark

4. A robin might wash in a (bird)bath.   bird

5. My new coat is (water)proof.   water

6. An (egg)shell is a bird's first home.   egg

Rhyming

Write the List Words that rhyme with the words given.

1. florist forest   4. twister sister

2. decide beside   5. prince since

3. wife life   6. white quite

Flex Your Spelling Muscles

Writing

Birds come in many colors, shapes, and sizes. Write a description of one or more birds you have seen or heard about. Include details, such as what they look and sound like. Use as many List Words as you can.

Proofreading

Each sentence below has two mistakes. Use the proofreading marks to fix the mistakes. Then write the misspelled List Words on the lines.

1. The hummingbird is the (berd) with the smallest (eeg.)

1. _bird egg_

2. a duck has feet shaped like paddles so it can swim in the (watter.)

2. _water_

3. Penguins canot fly, but they can swim (faste.)

3. _fast_

4. An eagle lives in the african rain (forrest.)

4. _forest_

Now proofread your description of birds. Fix any mistakes.

Go for the Goal

Take your Final Test. Then fill in your Scoreboard. Send your mistakes to the Word Locker.

SCOREBOARD

number correct	number wrong

★ ★ ★ ★ ★ ★ ★ ★ ★ **All-Star Words** ★ ★ ★ ★ ★ ★ ★ ★ ★

carpet   shirt   sidewalk   mile   canvas

Write a sentence for each word. Read each sentence aloud to a partner, leaving out the All-Star Word. Have your partner say the word that goes in the sentence.

Name _____

Consonants

Warm Up

How much does the heaviest cat weigh?

Cat Tales

There are about 40 million cats in North America. A few
are famous. You may have seen them on TV or in cartoons.
Here are **some** not-so-famous cats who could have been
prize winners.

The **prize** for "fat cat" goes to a cat in Connecticut.
Most cats weigh about ten pounds. This cat weighed
in at 43 pounds. That's heavier than **four** bowling
balls! "Fat cat" should have watched what it ate.

Speaking of eating, most cats like to catch a
mouse or two. The prize for "mouser" goes to Mickey.
He caught more than 22 thousand mice. It took
him a long time to make this record. For 23 years
he **was** the "house" cat for a company in England.
It is not known what this company made.
Perhaps it was cheese.

Two other "house" cats owned their own house.
They share the prize for "richest cats." The cats
belonged to a doctor in California. When he died, he
left them everything. It all came to $415, 000. That's a
lot of cat chow!

Say <u>prize</u> and <u>left</u>. How many consonants do you
hear? Say <u>was</u> and <u>perhaps</u>. How are the sounds
at the end of each word different?

On Your Mark

Take your Warm Up Test. Then check your spelling with
the List Words on the next page.

9

Pep Talk

A **consonant blend** is two or more consonants that come together in a word. Their sounds blend together, but each sound is heard, as in <u>prize</u> and <u>left</u>. The /z/ sound can be spelled with the letter **z**, as in <u>size</u>, or the letter **s**, as in <u>was</u>.

LIST WORDS

1. some   *some*
2. mostly   *mostly*
3. four   *four*
4. wore   *wore*
5. was   *was*
6. ground   *ground*
7. left   *left*
8. into   *into*
9. size   *size*
10. yell   *yell*
11. prize   *prize*
12. perhaps   *perhaps*
13. rise   *rise*
14. kept   *kept*
15. else   *else*

Game Plan

Spelling Lineup

Write each List Word under the correct heading. One word will be written twice.

/z/ sound spelled **s**	/z/ sound spelled **z**
1. was	3. size
2. rise	4. prize

Write the two List Words that rhyme with <u>pour</u>.

5. wore   6. four

Write the missing blends to finish List Words.

7. gr**ound**   10. pr**ize**

8. **ke**pt   11. **mo**stly

9. **le**ft

Write the missing consonants to finish List Words.

12. pe**rha**ps   15. ye**ll**

13. **i**n**to**   16. so**m**e

14. el**s**e

Vocabulary

Write the List Word that matches each clue.

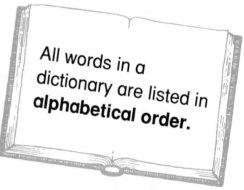

FIRST PRIZE

1. You do this when you want someone to hear you. _yell_

2. You win this in a contest. _prize_

3. You do this as you get up from your chair. _rise_

4. Two plus two equals this number. _four_

5. This is the soil or land you walk on. _ground_

6. This is another word for <u>maybe</u>. _perhapes_

Alphabetical Order

Write the List Words from the box in alphabetical order. When you write words in alphabetical order, use these rules:
1. If the first letter of two words is the same, use the second letter.
2. If the first two letters are the same, use the third letter.

All words in a dictionary are listed in **alphabetical order.**

kept	yell	else	size	into
left	was	wore	mostly	some

1. _else_   6. _size_

2. _into_   7. _some_

3. _kept_   8. _was_

4. _left_   9. _wore_

5. _mostly_   10. _yell_

Flex Your Spelling Muscles

Writing

Think of a cat you have seen in real life or on television that did something silly. Use the List Words to write a description about it.

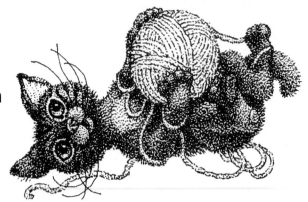

Proofreading

Each sentence has two mistakes. Use the proofreading marks to fix the mistakes. Write the misspelled List Words on the lines.

Proofreading Marks	
⬭	spelling mistake
⊙	add period

1. My cat wins the (prise) for high jumping⊙

2. He lands on all (foer) feet when he hits the (grownd.)

3. Sometimes he jumps (intoo) a tree ⊙

4. (Mostley) he jumps on tables and chairs ⊙

5. (Perrhaps) that is why he makes me (yeel.)

1. _prize_
2. _four_
   ground
3. _into_
4. _mostly_
5. _perhaps_
   yell

Now proofread your description. Fix any mistakes.

Go for the Goal

Take your Final Test. Then fill in your Scoreboard. Send your mistakes to the Word Locker.

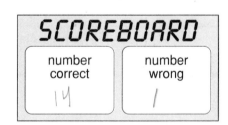

SCOREBOARD

number correct	number wrong
14	1

★ ★ ★ ★ ★ ★ ★ ★ **All-Star Words** ★ ★ ★ ★ ★ ★ ★ ★

promise   honest   gaze   grind   ashes

Write a sentence for each All-Star Word, but leave a blank in place of the word. Trade papers with a partner. Write the word that belongs in each blank.

Name _____

Hard and Soft c and g

Warm Up

How does Juan make a paper ladybug move?

Ladybug, Ladybug

Juan held a plain piece of paper up in front of his friends. He showed them that it was just an ordinary everyday piece of paper. Next he picked up a cut out drawing of a **giant** ladybug and placed it on the paper. Then he said, "Ladybug, ladybug, turn around." And like **magic**, the paper bug began to turn and move. Then he held up the sheet, and made the ladybug **climb** up. You should have seen his friends' **faces**.

How did he do it? Simple. Juan taped a paper clip to the underside of the bug. He held the sheet of paper with one hand, and in his other hand, he hid a small magnet. He moved the magnet around behind the sheet of paper. Now that you know how the trick is done, why not **give** it a try. Presto! You'll drive your friends buggy!

 Look back at the words in dark print. Say each word. What two sounds does the **c** make? What two sounds does the **g** make?

On Your Mark

Take your Warm Up Test. Then check your spelling with the List Words on the next page.

13

Pep Talk

The letter **c** can make a hard sound, as in <u>case</u> and a soft sound, as in <u>ice</u>.
The letter **g** can make a hard sound, as in <u>gone</u> and a soft sound, as in <u>cage</u>.

LIST WORDS

1. ice ✓ *ice*
2. pick ✓ *pick*
3. gone ✓ *gone*
4. case ✓ *case*
5. faces ✓ *faces*
6. cage ✓ *cage*
7. magic ✓ *magic*
8. age ✓ *age*
9. wagon ✓ *wagon*
10. give ✓ *give*
11. giant ✓ *giant*
12. once ✓ *once*
13. danger ✓ *danger*
14. places ✓ *places*
15. climb ✓ *climb*

Game Plan

Spelling Lineup

Write each List Word under the correct heading. Some words may be written twice.

hard c as in <u>car</u>

1. case
2. cage
3. climb
4. pick
5. magic

soft c as in <u>city</u>

9. ice
10. places
11. once
12. faces

hard g as in <u>game</u>

6. give
7. wagon
8. gone

soft g as in <u>page</u>

13. giant
14. age
15. danger
16. magic
17. gage

Vocabulary

Write the List Word that matches each clue.

1. It can carry a heavy load. _wagon_

2. A pet bird may live in this. _cage_

3. It will make your drink cold. _ice_

4. Tales may start, " ___ upon a time." _once_

5. This means the opposite of here. _gone_

6. These have eyes and mouths. _faces_

7. This is the opposite of take. _give_

8. This means to choose. _pick_

9. This means how old a person is. _age_

10. Presto! A rabbit's in my hat! _magic_

Puzzle

Write a List Word to complete each sentence. Then read down the shaded boxes to answer the riddle.

1. It takes strong legs to ___ a mountain.

2. Tom went to many ___ on his trip.

3. The sign said, " ___ ! Ice on Road!"

4. Jack climbed the beanstalk and met a ___ .

5. The bottles of juice came in a cardboard ___ .

c	l	i	m	b		
	p	l	a	c	e	s
d	a	n	g	e	r	
		G	i	a	n	t
		c	a	s	e	

Riddle: What would you need to take an elephant for a ride on your bike?

Answer: w a g o n

Flex Your Spelling Muscles

Writing

What magic tricks have you seen? Maybe you know how to do a magic trick yourself. Use the List Words to write directions telling how it's done.

MAGIC SHOW TODAY

Proofreading

Each sentence below has two mistakes. Use the proofreading marks to fix the mistakes. Write the misspelled List Words on the lines.

Proofreading Marks	
⬭	spelling mistake
≡	capital letter

1. the magician asked Roy to pik a card.

2. he put Roy's card in a hat and waved a majic wand.

3. now he will giv the hat a tap.

4. suddenly, the card is gon!

5. did you see the surprise on all the people's fases?

1. _pick_

2. _magic_

3. _give_

4. _gone_

5. _faces_

Now proofread your directions. Fix any mistakes.

Go for the Goal

Take your Final Test. Then fill in your Scoreboard. Send your mistakes to the Word Locker.

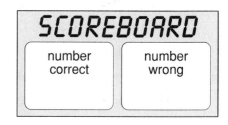

SCOREBOARD

number correct	number wrong

★ ★ ★ ★ ★ ★ ★ ★ ★ **All-Star Words** ★ ★ ★ ★ ★ ★ ★ ★ ★

cargo   garage   glisten   pack   exercise

Write what you think each All-Star Word means. Then check the definitions in your dictionary. Trade papers with a partner. Write the All-Star Word that goes with each meaning.

Name _____

Short-Vowel Sounds

Warm Up

Where does the anglerfish keep its fishing line?

Something Fishy

Have you ever heard of an "anglerfish"? An "angler" is a person who fishes with a line and hook. If you think an anglerfish is a fish that goes fishing, you're close. It **does** go fishing—with its own line and bait.

This strange fish does not "fish" in the usual way. It does not hang its line down into the water. It does its fishing from the **bottom** of the ocean. The anglerfish stays deep **under** the water. Like a **rock** on the ocean floor, it doesn't move. It does look up. **Its** eyes are on top of its head. Its fishing lines are on its head, too! These float up through the water. When fish swimming **past** think they see worms, they come closer. The anglerfish doesn't need a hook to catch **them**. It has a very large jaw. When the fish swim by to eat the "worms," the anglerfish will just **gobble** them up.

 Say each word in dark print. What vowel sounds do you hear?

On Your Mark

Take your Warm Up Test. Then check your spelling with the List Words on the next page.

Pep Talk

The vowels are **a, e, i, o, u,** and sometimes **y** and **w**. Every syllable in a word has a vowel sound. <u>Rock</u> has one vowel sound. <u>Bottom</u> has two. Short-vowel sounds are often spelled with just the vowel sound itself, but:
short **e** in <u>dead</u> is spelled **ea**, and
short **u** in <u>does</u> is spelled **oe**.

LIST WORDS

1. little *little*
2. its *its*
3. under *under*
4. rock *rock*
5. dead *dead*
6. past *past*
7. them *them*
8. collar *collar*
9. dug *dug*
10. does *does*
11. gobble *gobble*
12. bottom *bottom*
13. level *level*
14. felt *felt*
15. next *next*

Game Plan

Spelling Lineup

Write the List Words that have one syllable.

1. _____   6. _____

2. _____   7. _____

3. _____   8. _____

4. _____   9. _____

5. _____

Write the List Words that have two syllables.

10. _____   13. _____

11. _____   14. _____

12. _____   15. _____

Dictionary

Each List Word below has been divided into syllables. Say each word. Put an accent mark (´) after the syllable with the strong sound. Then write the List Word.

In a dictionary, an **accent mark** appears after the syllable with the strong sound.
lit´ tle

1. col lar _____

2. un der _____

3. bot tom _____

4. gob ble _____

5. lev el _____

Scrambled Letters Puzzle

Unscramble the letters to spell List Words. Print one letter in each box. Then read down the shaded boxes to answer the riddle.

1. SIT

2. XENT

3. DADE

4. CKOR

5. TELF

6. TILLTE

7. STAP

8. MHET

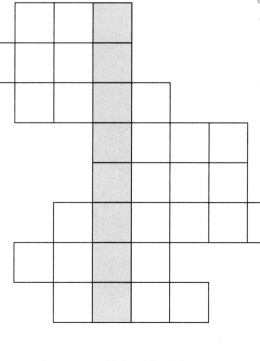

Riddle: What is the most famous fish of all?

Answer: a ___ ___ ___ ___ ___ ___ ___

Flex Your Spelling Muscles

Writing

Have you ever seen a strange fish, bug, or other animal? Write a poem telling about a real animal or a made up one. Use as many List Words as you can.

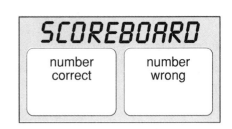

Proofreading

Each sentence below has two mistakes. Use the proofreading marks to fix the mistakes. Write the misspelled List Words on the lines.

Proofreading Marks	
⬭	spelling mistake
⊙	add period

1. A flounder fish lives on the ocean bottum

1. _____

2. It dus look strange because both itz eyes are on the same side of its head.

2. _____

_____

3. The flat flounder lies levil with the sand

3. _____

4. It lies uhnder sand that it has duge up.

4. _____

_____

5. Flounders can be colored like a rok on top

5. _____

6. People like thim because they are tasty

6. _____

Now proofread your animal poem. Fix any mistakes.

Go for the Goal

Take your Final Test. Then fill in your Scoreboard. Send your mistakes to the Word Locker.

SCOREBOARD

number correct	number wrong

★ ★ ★ ★ ★ ★ ★ ★ **All-Star Words** ★ ★ ★ ★ ★ ★ ★ ★

tender   lack   humble   chop   instead

Write a sentence for each word, then scramble the letters in the All-Star Words. Trade papers with a partner. Unscramble each other's words.

Long-Vowel Sounds

Warm Up

What kind of jam won't spread on bread?

A Squiggly Tale

You can believe it or not, but last week the Landview Police Department got a call from a Mrs. Sadie Rose, who was very upset. Mrs. Sadie Rose said that there was a pig causing a **huge** traffic jam on the main road through town. Traffic was blocked for miles.

A police unit, with siren wailing, drove to the scene. When they arrived, they found a pig standing in the middle of the **street**. An officer neared the pig carefully. "What are you doing here?" asked the officer. "I'm on my way to the market," answered the pig.

"Sir, roads are for cars to **drive** on," said the officer.

"I **know**," answered the pig.

"Sir, only people in cars are allowed on the highway," said the officer.

The pig looked very insulted. "I have every right to be here," replied the pig. "After all, I am a road hog."

Personally, I don't believe it!

Say each word in dark print in the selection. What vowel sound do you hear in each word?

On Your Mark

Take your Warm Up Test. Then check your spelling with the List Words on the next page.

21

A **long-vowel sound** often has the same sound as its letter name, but long-vowel sounds can be spelled many ways.
For example:
long **a** in <u>raise</u> is spelled **ai**
long **e** in <u>seat</u> is spelled **ea.**
The sound-symbols for long-vowels are:
a = /ā/ e = /ē/ i = /ī/ o = /ō/ u = /yōō/

LIST WORDS

1. hello *hello*
2. raise *raise*
3. drive *drive*
4. huge *huge*
5. lines *lines*
6. blame *blame*
7. street *street*
8. seat *seat*
9. fumes *fumes*
10. know *know*
11. only *only*
12. people *people*
13. steel *steel*
14. mail *mail*
15. used *used*

Game Plan

Spelling Lineup

Write each List Word under the correct heading. One word will be used twice.

/ā/

1. _____
2. _____
3. _____

/ī/

4. _____
5. _____

/ō/

6. _____
7. _____
8. _____

/ē/

9. _____
10. _____
11. _____
12. _____
13. _____

/yōō/

14. _____
15. _____
16. _____

Missing Words

Write a List Word to finish each sentence.

1. Our teacher will _____ the answer to this question.

2. The smell of the paint _____ is strong.

3. Look both ways before you cross the _____ .

4. The bus driver will _____ you to school.

5. Most bridges today are made of strong _____ .

6. Students _____ their hands to ask a question.

7. Hannah _____ a rubber patch to fix my tire.

8. Please put a stamp on this letter before you _____ it.

Puzzle

Fill in the crossword puzzle by writing a List Word to answer each clue.

ACROSS
3. a road
4. very, very big
5. to say someone did
   something bad
6. rows of persons
   or things
7. another word for just

DOWN
1. to lift up
2. men, women,
   and children
3. a chair or bench
4. a greeting

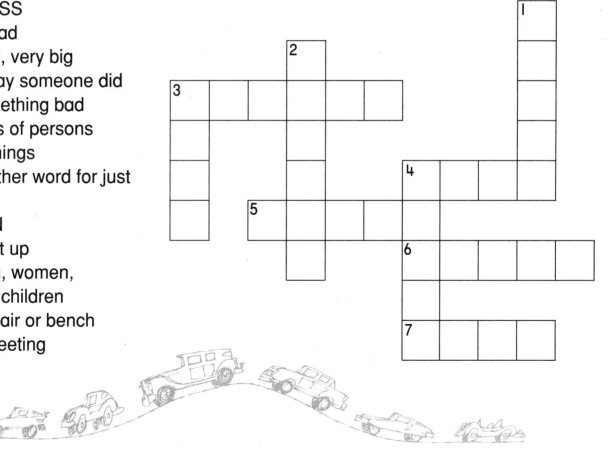

Flex Your Spelling Muscles

Writing

Use the List Words to write a joke or riddle you know.
For example: Why did the chicken cross the <u>street</u>?
Answer: To get to the other side. Then try out
your joke on a friend.

Proofreading

Each sentence below has two mistakes. Use the
proofreading marks to fix the mistakes. Write the
misspelled List Words on the lines.

Proofreading Marks	
⬭	spelling mistake
≡	capital letter

1. have you heard the joke that peeple tell about
   an elephant?

2. i've onley heard it once, so tell me again.

3. how do you knoe when an elephant has been in
   the refrigerator?

4. there will be a huje footprint in the butter.

1. _____

2. _____

3. _____

4. _____

Now proofread your joke or riddle. Fix any mistakes.

Go for the Goal

Take your Final Test. Then fill in your Scoreboard.
Send your mistakes to the Word Locker.

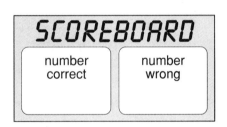

★ ★ ★ ★ ★ ★ ★ ★ **All-Star Words** ★ ★ ★ ★ ★ ★ ★ ★

weak   drain   device   fold   usually

Write a sentence for each All-Star Word. Trade papers with a
partner. Circle the letters that stand for the long-vowel sounds in
the All-Star Words.

Instant Replay • Lessons 1–5

Time Out

Take another look at consonant sounds and blends, the hard and soft sounds of **c** and **g**, and words with short- and long-vowel sounds.

Check Your Word Locker

Look at the words in your Word Locker. Write the troublesome words for Lessons 1 through 5.

_____

_____

Practice writing your troublesome words with a partner. Take turns writing each word as the other slowly spells it aloud.

Lesson 1

The **vowels** in the alphabet are **a**, **e**, **i**, **o**, **u**, and sometimes **y** and **w**. All the other letters are **consonants.**

List Words
bird
sister
quite
nine
mark
fast

Each riddle has an answer with rhyming words in it. Write a List Word to finish each answer.

1. What color is paper?

   _____ white

2. What is an ink blot?

   a dark _____

3. What is next to the second hen?

   a third _____

4. Where is that name?

   on line _____

5. What is a quick boom?

   a _____ blast

6. How did Mom greet a family member?

   kissed her _____

25

Consonants may blend together, as they do in <u>ground</u> and <u>prize</u>. Listen for the two sounds made by the letter **s**, as in <u>was</u> and <u>perhaps</u>.

List Words
some
was
rise
mostly
size
else

Write each List Word under the sound you hear in it.

both /s/ and /z/

1. _____

/z/

2. _____

3. _____

/s/

4. _____

5. _____

6. _____

Lesson 3

Listen for the hard and soft sounds of the letters **c** and **g**, as in <u>case</u>, <u>ice</u>, <u>age</u>, and <u>gone</u>.

List Words
cage
give
once
wagon
giant
danger

Write the List Word that goes with each clue.

1. has wheels

   _____

2. pet bird's house

   _____

3. threat

   _____

4. hand to someone

   _____

5. only one time

   _____

6. huge

   _____

Short-vowel sounds are often spelled with just the vowel itself, as in <u>dug</u>. Notice the different spellings of the short-vowel sounds in <u>does</u> and <u>dead</u>.

List Words

under
collar
does
dead
bottom
level

Write the List Words in alphabetical order.

1. _____   6. _____

2. _____

3. _____

4. _____

5. _____

Long-vowel sounds have the same sound as their letter names, but long-vowel sounds can be spelled many ways, as in <u>street</u>, <u>seat</u>, <u>know</u>, and <u>mail</u>.

List Words

raise
know
people
huge
mail
only

Circle each List Word that is misspelled. Then write it on the line correctly.

1. You know all the poeple in this room. _____

2. We have a huje dog named Dinosaur. _____

3. Please raize your hand before you speak. _____

4. I can stay onlly a few days. _____

5. Everyone will knoe the words to this song. _____

6. I see a huge pile of mial on the table. _____

List Words

only
mostly
giant
huge
bird
danger
people
raise
once
under

Circle the word that does not make sense in each sentence. Then choose the List Word that makes better sense in the sentence and write it on the line.

1. There is a board in the tree. _____

2. The bear is hug. _____

3. I saw a giraffe mountain. _____

4. I am the onion child in my family. _____

5. Worm upon a time, a frog met a prince. _____

6. I will raisin the blinds. _____

7. Many peaches live in the city. _____

8. The daisy passed, so I felt safer. _____

9. A river flows uncle the bridge. _____

10. I moose like to read mysteries. _____

Go for the Goal

Take your Final Replay Test. Then fill in your Scoreboard. Send any misspelled words to your Word Locker.

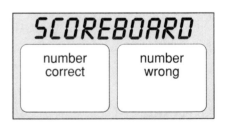

SCOREBOARD

number correct	number wrong

ground
cannot
gobble
climb
fumes

Clean Out Your Word Locker

Look in your Word Locker. Cross out each word you spelled correctly on your Final Replay Test. Circle the words you're still having trouble with. Add the words you circled to your Spelling Notebook. What do you notice about the words? Watch for those words as you write.

Long-Vowel Sounds

Warm Up

What kind of store is in this building?

Musical Art

This wall is **alive** with the sight of **music!** Music is a tune that you can hear, isn't it? Yes, but you can see music, too. You can see the notes that a music writer puts on paper for other people to sing or play.

The tune on this wall has to be one of the world's largest. It's like a giant **page** of music. Is it the work of a songwriter who likes to paint? Is it the **crazy joke** of some singing sign painter? No, it is a mural, which is a special kind of painting done on a wall. This mural is five stories high! Why would anyone put so much music on the side of a building? Can you guess? **Inside** the building is a music store.

You can see this song on a building in the city of Minneapolis. If you can **read** music, you may even like to sing or play the song.

Say each word in dark print in the selection. Listen for the long-vowel sounds. What do you notice about the ways the long-vowel sounds are spelled?

On Your Mark

Take your Warm Up Test. Then check your spelling with the List Words on the next page.

Words with long-vowel sounds can have different spelling patterns. The **ea** in break spells /ā/. The **ea** in team spells /ē/. The **ea** in read can spell /ē/ or /e/. Look at how the long-vowel sound is spelled in each List Word.

LIST WORDS

1. alive   *alive*
2. human   *human*
3. page   *page*
4. joke   *joke*
5. grind   *grind*
6. inside   *inside*
7. read   *read*
8. seen   *seen*
9. load   *load*
10. music   *music*
11. crazy   *crazy*
12. break   *break*
13. team   *team*
14. east   *east*
15. stone   *stone*

Game Plan

Spelling Lineup

Write each List Word under the correct heading.

/ā/ as in <u>day</u>

1. _____
2. _____
3. _____

/ō/ as in <u>glow</u>

11. _____
12. _____
13. _____

/ē/ as in <u>free</u>

4. _____
5. _____
6. _____
7. _____

/yoo/ as in <u>huge</u>

14. _____
15. _____

/ī/ as in <u>side</u>

8. _____
9. _____
10. _____

Alphabetical Order

Circle the List Words that are hiding in the puzzle. Look across and down. Write the List Words in alphabetical order.

```
S   H   U   M   A   N   O   T
G   L   E   U   C   N   L   E
R   X   A   S   E   E   N   A
I   N   S   I   D   E   C   M
N   S   T   C   R   A   Z   Y
D   P   A   B   R   E   A   K
```

1. _____
2. _____
3. _____
4. _____
5. _____
6. _____
7. _____
8. _____
9. _____

Missing Words

Write a List Word from the box to finish each answer.

alive	page	load	stone	read	joke

1. Why are you laughing? She told a _____ .

2. Where is the name of this book's publisher?

   It is on the title _____ .

3. Why do you water your plants? It keeps them _____ .

4. How will you move the furniture?

   I will _____ it into a truck.

5. What will you use to build that wall?

   I'll use a special kind of hard _____ .

6. What will you do with that magazine?

   I think I'll _____ it.

Flex Your Spelling Muscles

Writing

How do you feel about music? Do you find yourself humming tunes or singing songs? Use the List Words to write a paragraph telling what kind of music you like and why.

Proofreading

Each sentence below has two mistakes. Use the proofreading marks to fix each mistake. Write the misspelled List Words on the lines.

Proofreading Marks

⬭ spelling mistake

∧ add something

1. Have you sean the dancers on stage

1. _____

2. They are the best dance teem alliv.

2. _____

_____

3. The musik they use sounds wild and crazee.

3. _____

_____

4. Did you rede about them in the newspaper

4. _____

5. There is a story about the dancers inscid on the second paje.

5. _____

_____

Now proofread your paragraph about music. Fix any mistakes.

Go for the Goal

Take your Final Test. Then fill in your Scoreboard. Send your mistakes to the Word Locker.

SCOREBOARD

number correct	number wrong

★ ★ ★ ★ ★ ★ ★ ★ ★ **All-Star Words** ★ ★ ★ ★ ★ ★ ★ ★ ★

erase   pirate   ruler   coach   release

Write a sentence for each word. Read the sentences to your partner, but say *blank* in place of the All-Star Words. Have your partner write the missing words.

Name —————————————————————————

Consonant Blends

Warm Up

Is a smile or a frown easier for your face to make?

Put on a Happy Face

The more you crack it the more people will like it. That's what a **smile** is all about. Did you know that **frowning** is harder than smiling? A frown uses 43 of the muscles in your face. It takes only 17 muscles to smile. So it's easy. Put on a happy face, and make some new **friends**.

Smiling is good for your health, too. Doctors and many other **smart** people believe that laughing helps sick people feel better inside. The laughing makes their bodies get well, too! **Best** of all, a smile is **free!**

So don't be **blind** to the fact that it's easier to smile than to frown. It's the doctor's orders!

Say each word in dark print in the selection. What consonant sounds do you hear at the beginning of the words. What consonant sounds do you hear at the end of <u>best</u>?

On Your Mark

Take your Warm Up Test. Then check your spelling with the List Words on the next page.

A **consonant blend** is two or more consonants that come together in a word. Their sounds blend together, but each sound is heard. Each List Word has an **s, l,** or **r** blend at the beginning or at the end of the word, or at the beginning and at the end.

LIST WORDS

1. smile   *smile*
2. smart   *smart*
3. best   *best*
4. free   *free*
5. spend   *spend*
6. blind   *blind*
7. float   *float*
8. plant   *plant*
9. slumber   *slumber*
10. sting   *sting*
11. frowning   *frowning*
12. friends   *friends*
13. creek   *creek*
14. glue   *glue*
15. bring   *bring*

Game Plan

Spelling Lineup

Write the List Words that begin or end with **s** blends.

1. _____   4. _____
2. _____   5. _____
3. _____   6. _____

Write the List Words that begin with **r** blends.

7. _____   10. _____
8. _____   11. _____
9. _____

Write the List Words that begin with **l** blends.

12. _____
13. _____
14. _____
15. _____
16. _____

Rhyming

Write the List Words that rhyme with the words given.

1. west _____

2. boat _____

3. sneak _____

4. number _____

5. part _____

6. clowning _____

Scrambled Letters Puzzle

Unscramble the letters to spell List Words. Print one letter in each box. Then read down the shaded boxes to answer the riddle.

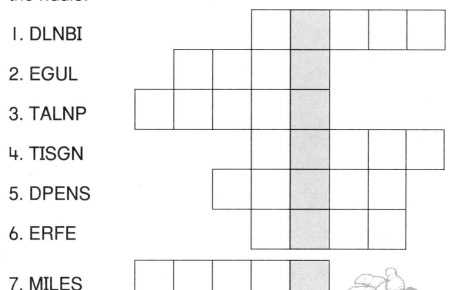

1. DLNBI

2. EGUL

3. TALNP

4. TISGN

5. DPENS

6. ERFE

7. MILES

Riddle: What is at the beginning of everything,
At the end of every mile,
At the beginning of every end,
And at the end of every smile?

Answer: It is the _____ _____ .

Flex Your Spelling Muscles

Writing

What makes you laugh? How does laughing make you feel? Write a brief paragraph that describes your feelings. Use as many List Words as you can.

Proofreading

Each sentence below has two mistakes. Use the proofreading marks to fix each mistake. Write the misspelled List Words on the lines.

Proofreading Marks	
⬭	spelling mistake
≡	capital letter
⊙	add period

1. my family will spende Saturday at the circus.

2. I get to bering my freands with me.

3. children get in frea that day.

4. No frouning allowed when you see the clowns

5. Those trained elephants are really snart

6. we all smyile when we see the lions.

1. _____

2. _____

   _____

3. _____

4. _____

5. _____

6. _____

Now proofread your paragraph. Fix any mistakes.

Go for the Goal

Take your Final Test. Then fill in your Scoreboard. Send your mistakes to the Word Locker.

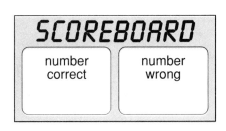

SCOREBOARD

number correct	number wrong

★ ★ ★ ★ ★ ★ ★ ★ **All-Star Words** ★ ★ ★ ★ ★ ★ ★ ★

crack   stem   glide   blast   freeze

Write a sentence using each All-Star Word. Trade sentences with a partner. Circle the All-Star Words in the sentences.

Name —————————————————————————

Consonant Blends

Warm Up

What is the annual Cowboy Poetry Gathering?

Poetry Round Up

Every year, thousands of gals and guys **plan** a **trip** to a small Nevada town for a different **kind** of rodeo. It's a rodeo of rhyme called the annual Cowboy Poetry Gathering. This **special** event brings together cowpokes who not only enjoy poetry, but also enjoy life on the open range! They gather to recite the rhymes they've written during the year on the wild prairie. Here's a sample of their kind of poetic horseplay:

To My Horse, Whinny

There are other colts in my corral,
Among them you're the best.
You're faithful, loyal, my best pal,
And hooves beyond the rest!
> Of all the ponies in the race,
> I'm sure that you would beat 'em
> I'd really like to bring you **flowers**,
> But I know you'd only eat 'em.
>> And I will love you for all time,
>> I'm stating here and now.
>> I'm writing you this round up rhyme,
>> 'Cause you're prettier than a cow.

 Look back at the words in dark print. Can you name the consonant blend in each word?

On Your Mark

Take your Warm Up Test. Then check your spelling with the List Words on the next page.

LIST WORDS

1. trip — *trip*
2. drove — *drove*
3. plan — *plan*
4. kind — *kind*
5. floors — *floors*
6. melting — *melting*
7. blaze — *blaze*
8. spill — *spill*
9. flowers — *flowers*
10. Friday — *Friday*
11. frozen — *frozen*
12. please — *please*
13. broken — *broken*
14. fresh — *fresh*
15. special — *special*

Game Plan

Spelling Lineup

Write the List Words under the headings. Circle the consonant blend in each word. Remember that **sh** and **ng** are not consonant blends.

one syllable

1. _____   6. _____
2. _____   7. _____
3. _____   8. _____
4. _____   9. _____
5. _____

two syllables

10. _____   15. _____
11. _____
12. _____
13. _____
14. _____

Alphabetical Order

Write each group of List Words in alphabetical order.

please	1. _____
broken	2. _____
kind	3. _____
plan	4. _____

melting	1. _____
floors	2. _____
spill	3. _____
fresh	4. _____

Missing Words

Write List Words to finish the story. The word shapes will help you.

[_____] was a [_____] day.

Dad [_____] us to the lake. The lake was

[_____]. Inside the cabin, Mom and I lit a fire. In the

morning, the ice on the lake was [_____]. We even

saw pretty purple [_____] peeping through the snow.

Flex Your Spelling Muscles

Writing

Poems can be serious or funny. They can rhyme or not rhyme. Poems can be just about anything you want them to be. Use the List Words to write a poem of your own.

Proofreading

Each sentence below has two mistakes. Use the proofreading marks to fix each mistake. Write the misspelled List Words on the lines.

Proofreading Marks
⬭ spelling mistake
˅ add apostrophe

1. We took a tripp west in Dads new car.

2. On Fridae we droev through the mountains.

3. It was so cold my sisters face felt frosen.

4. Our plann was to stop at my aunts ranch.

5. When we got there, there was a freash blaiz in the fireplace.

1. _____

2. _____

   _____

3. _____

4. _____

5. _____

   _____

Now proofread your poem. Fix any mistakes.

Go for the Goal

Take your Final Test. Then fill in your Scoreboard. Send your mistakes to the Word Locker.

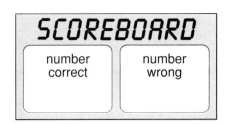

SCOREBOARD
| number correct | number wrong |

★ ★ ★ ★ ★ ★ ★ ★ ★ **All-Star Words** ★ ★ ★ ★ ★ ★ ★ ★ ★

treasure   plane   depend   spare   frost

Write a story using all the All-Star Words. Then erase two or three letters out of each All-Star Word. Trade papers with a partner. Fill in the missing letters.

Name _____

y as a Vowel

Warm Up

When is a dog not really a dog?

Prairie Pups

They look like squirrels, but they bark like little dogs. They play in fields, but stay under the ground at night. They have grayish brown coats, and they're cute. What are they? They're prairie dogs!

It seems as if these **playful** little animals have **always** been around. They have been seen popping out of holes since the days when North America was being settled. Although we call them dogs, they are really ground squirrels. They live together in a large group called a village, deep under the ground. Digging room after room, they make space for their **very** large **family**. A village can have more than a thousand prairie dogs in it. There are prairie dog villages all through the plains of North America from Mexico to Canada.

Prairie dogs eat grass and roots and can cause **plenty** of trouble for farmers. In fact, these **hungry** animals eat so many plants, they hardly ever need water. They get enough water from the plants. **Maybe** you'll find this hard to believe, but think about it this way. Has a prairie dog ever asked you for a drink of water?

Look back at the words in dark print. What do you notice about their spelling? Say each word. What vowel sound does the **y** stand for in each word?

On Your Mark

Take your Warm Up Test. Then check your spelling with the List Words on the next page.

In some words **y** teams up with **a** to spell /ā/, as in <u>maybe</u>. At the end of a word with more than one syllable, **y** may spell /ē/, as in <u>pretty</u>. Listen for the sound that **y** makes in each List Word.

LIST WORDS

1. lady *lady*
2. playful *playful*
3. always *always*
4. very *very*
5. empty *empty*
6. angry *angry*
7. any *any*
8. anyway *anyway*
9. maybe *maybe*
10. carry *carry*
11. family *family*
12. pretty *pretty*
13. plenty *plenty*
14. heavy *heavy*
15. hungry *hungry*

Game Plan

Spelling Lineup

Write the List Words in which **y** spells the final sound /ē/.

1. _____ 7. _____

2. _____ 8. _____

3. _____ 9. _____

4. _____ 10. _____

5. _____ 11. _____

6. _____

Write the List Words in which **ay** spells /ā/.

12. _____ 14. _____

13. _____ 15. _____

Dictionary

Each List Word below has been divided into syllables. Say each word. Put an accent mark (´) after the syllable with the strong sound. Then write the List Words.

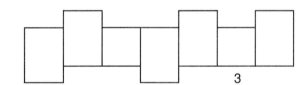

In a dictionary an **accent mark** appears after the syllable with the strong sound.
plen´ ty

1. ver y _____

2. la dy _____

3. car ry _____

4. an y _____

5. may be _____

6. fam i ly _____

7. an gry _____

8. hun gry _____

9. an y way _____

10. emp ty _____

Word Shape Puzzle

Write a List Word in each word shape.

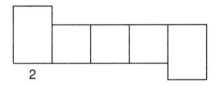

2

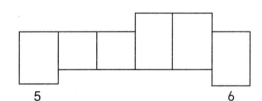

3

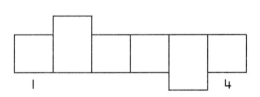

1

4

5

6

Use the number code to answer the riddle. Find the letter in the box with the number I under it. Print that letter on every line below that has the number I under it. Do the same for numbers 2 through 6.

Riddle: What do you call a quiet little dog?

Answer: ___ ___ ___ ___ ___   ___ ___ ___ ___ ___
        I   2 3 4 2   5 3 5 5 6

Flex Your Spelling Muscles

Writing

The prairie dog villages and colorful flowers make the prairie a very interesting place. Write a description of where you live, a playground, or your favorite park. Tell what you would see, hear, or smell in that place. Try to use as many List Words as you can.

Proofreading

Each sentence has two mistakes. Use the proofreading marks to fix each mistake. Write the misspelled List Words on the lines.

Proofreading Marks
◯ spelling mistake
🖎 take out something

1. Prairie dogs can be playfulle, but they work vary hard, too.

1. _____

   _____

2. A prairie dog allwaes starts its home by digging a a tunnel.

2. _____

3. At the end of of the tunnel, mayby it'll make a sleeping room.

3. _____

4. It puts plente of food in another room to keep for the the winter.

4. _____

Now proofread your description. Fix any mistakes.

Go for the Goal

Take your Final Test. Then fill in your Scoreboard. Send your mistakes to the Word Locker.

SCOREBOARD

number correct	number wrong

★ ★ ★ ★ ★ ★ ★ ★ ★ **All-Star Words** ★ ★ ★ ★ ★ ★ ★ ★ ★

holiday   sixty   country   easy   Monday

Write a sentence for each word, but leave a blank for the All-Star Word that completes the sentence. Trade papers with a partner. See if you can write the correct word in each sentence.

Name _____

y as a Vowel

LESSON
11

Warm Up

What kind of things have people used as money?

Funny Money

Money hasn't always been the coins and bills we have today. At one time or another, almost anything could be used for money. In fact, money can be anything people use to **buy** and sell things. Three hundred years ago, the Russians used leather for money. In China, tea was used. At one time, salt paid for things in parts of Africa. People have traded with gunpowder, cows, and even the jawbones of pigs! The island of Manhattan in New York City was bought by the Dutch from some Native Americans. The Native Americans were paid in glass beads. That was in 1626. Today, people use paper money printed by their governments.

Many board games use "play" money. Believe it or not, **every** year the play money printed for these games comes to more than all the real money printed in the world. Don't get any funny ideas or try to be **sly**. Can you guess what will happen if **anyone** tries to spend it?

Look back at the words in dark print. Say each word. What vowel sound does the **y** spell or help to spell in each word?

On Your Mark

Take your Warm Up Test. Then check your spelling with the List Words on the next page.

45

LIST WORDS

1. army — *army*
2. anyone — *anyone*
3. twenty — *twenty*
4. shy — *shy*
5. candy — *candy*
6. dry — *dry*
7. body — *body*
8. money — *money*
9. buy — *buy*
10. honey — *honey*
11. every — *every*
12. eye — *eye*
13. sly — *sly*
14. turkey — *turkey*
15. chimney — *chimney*

Game Plan

Spelling Lineup

Write the List Words in which **y** spells or helps to spell /ē/.

1. _____
2. _____
3. _____
4. _____
5. _____
6. _____
7. _____
8. _____
9. _____
10. _____

Write the List Words in which **y** spells or helps to spell /ī/.

11. _____
12. _____
13. _____
14. _____
15. _____

Scrambled Letters

Unscramble the letters to make List Words.

1. HYS   _____

2. YEOHN _____

3. YEE   _____

4. REVEY _____

5. RYD   _____

6. TNWYTE _____

7. YUB   _____

8. AENOYN _____

9. HICEYNM _____

10. BOYD _____

Definitions

Write the List Word that matches the meaning given.

1. a large group of soldiers   _____

2. a sweet food   _____

3. any person   _____

4. a big bird   _____

5. the main part of a person or animal _____

6. a pipe used to release smoke   _____

Flex Your Spelling Muscles

Writing

If you could choose one thing to use instead of money, what would it be? Write a paragraph to convince others that your form of money is the best. Use as many List Words as you can.

Proofreading

Each sentence below has two mistakes. Use the proofreading marks to fix each mistake. Write the misspelled List Words on the lines.

Proofreading Marks	
⬭	spelling mistake
⊙	add period
∧	add something

1. At one time, people used shells as monee

2. Rare feathers and huney were used in trade

3. Who hadthe sliy idea to use paper?

4. Would my turkee feather beworth something?

1. _____

2. _____

3. _____

4. _____

Now proofread your paragraph. Fix any mistakes.

Go for the Goal

Take your Final Test. Then fill in your Scoreboard. Send your mistakes to the Word Locker.

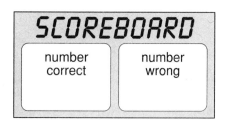

SCOREBOARD

number correct	number wrong

★ ★ ★ ★ ★ ★ ★ ★ ★ **All-Star Words** ★ ★ ★ ★ ★ ★ ★ ★ ★

aye   spy   hockey   everybody   anyhow

Use the All-Star Words to create a crossword puzzle. Draw a grid and write a clue for each word. Swap papers with a partner. Can you fill in the puzzle with the correct All-Star Words?

Instant Replay • Lessons 7–11

Time Out

Take another look at words with long-vowel sounds, consonant blends, and **y** as a vowel.

Check Your Word Locker

Look at the words in your Word Locker. Which words for Lessons 7 through 11 did you have the most trouble with? Write them here.

_____

_____

Practice writing your troublesome words with a partner. Try writing invisible letters for each word with your finger on your partner's back. Your partner can spell the word aloud as you write.

Lesson 7

The vowels have long and short sounds. Long-vowel sounds can be spelled more than one way, as in <u>load</u> and <u>joke</u>.

List Words
alive
human
music
crazy
break
team

Write a List Word that means the same or almost the same as each word given.

1. crack _____

2. living _____

3. group _____

4. person _____

5. foolish _____

6. tune _____

Consonants can be alone or come together in a word. In a **consonant blend**, you can hear the sound of each letter. Listen for the consonant blends in smart, glue, and free.

List Words

smile
best
spend
float
friends
bring

Write a List Word that means the opposite of each word or phrase given.

1. sink _____   4. frown _____

2. worst _____   5. save _____

3. take away _____   6. enemies _____

You can hear the sounds of two or more letters together in a **consonant blend.** Listen for the blends in trip, plan, spill, and kind.

List Words

kind
floors
blaze
Friday
please
special

Write a List Word that matches each clue.

1. are walked on _____

2. not like all the rest _____

3. sweet and nice _____

4. nice word when you ask _____

5. the last day of the school week _____

6. what a fire is _____

In some words, **y** helps to spell /ā/, as in <u>playful</u>. The letter **y** may also spell /ē/ at the end of a word with more than one syllable, as in <u>pretty</u>.

List Words

always
anyway
maybe
family
heavy
hungry

One word is misspelled in each set of List Words. Circle the word that is wrong. Then write it correctly on the line.

1. anyway heavy famly _____

2. allways maybe anyway _____

3. hungry haevy family _____

4. always maybe aneyway _____

5. family hungery always _____

6. heavy maybee hungry _____

The letter **y** can spell /ī/ at the end of one-syllable words, as in <u>shy</u>. At the end of a word with more than one syllable, **y** can spell /ē/, as in <u>body</u>.

List Words

anyone
twenty
candy
money
buy
turkey

Write a List Word that rhymes with each word given.

1. twenty-one _____

2. plenty _____

3. jerky _____

4. sandy _____

5. my _____

6. honey _____

List Words

human
anyone
maybe
special
buy
music
family
please
money
always
friends
heavy

Write the List Word that matches the meaning given.

1. not like others _____

2. a person _____

3. weighing very much _____

4. relatives _____

5. people you know and like _____

6. any person _____

7. to get by paying money _____

8. series of pleasing sounds _____

9. perhaps _____

10. satisfy _____

11. at all times _____

12. coins or paper bills _____

Go for the Goal

Take your Final Replay Test. Then fill in your Scoreboard. Send any misspelled words to your Word Locker.

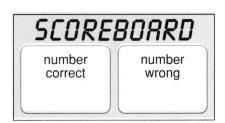

SCOREBOARD

number correct	number wrong

Clean Out Your Word Locker

Look in your Word Locker. Cross out each word you spelled correctly on your Final Replay Test. Circle the words you're still having trouble with. Add the words you circled to your Spelling Notebook. What do you notice about the words? Watch for those words as you write.

Vowels with r

Warm Up

What has one thousand heads?

A Green Giant

What is red and green and has a thousand heads? Give up? It's one of the world's biggest salads. At least the people of Milford, Massachusetts, say it was the biggest. They tossed their giant salad for Milford's bicentennial. That was the **year** that Milford had its 200th birthday. The people in Milford **care** a lot about their town. They wanted to make something really **large** so everyone would notice it.

The people had to **start** planning months **before** the big day. First, they had to **order** all the things to go into the salad. Then, for hours and hours, they chopped and sliced everything. When they were finished, their salad stretched out as long as a football field. It had one thousand heads of lettuce and tons of tomatoes, olives, cheese, peppers, and onions. There were gallons of dressing to go with it, too.

On the day of the **party,** each guest lined up with a fork and plate in hand. Then the mighty salad disappeared like magic. No one in Milford is sure if it was really the world's biggest salad, but for them, it was quite a mouthful!

Look back at the words in dark print in the selection. Say each word. What do you notice about the way the vowels sound in each word?

On Your Mark

Take your Warm Up Test. Then check your spelling with the List Words on the next page.

When a vowel comes before the letter **r** in a word, the sound of the vowel can change. Each List Word contains one of the vowel sounds represented by these sound-symbols:

/är/ as in <u>start</u>   /ir/ as in <u>year</u>

/ôr/ as in <u>fork</u>   /er/ as in <u>chair</u>

LIST WORDS

1. year *year*
2. care *care*
3. large *large*
4. start *start*
5. before *before*
6. order *order*
7. party *party*
8. fork *fork*
9. cheer *cheer*
10. chair *chair*
11. garden *garden*
12. morning *morning*
13. compare *compare*
14. clear *clear*
15. appear *appear*

Game Plan

Spelling Lineup

Write each List Word under the correct heading.

/är/ as in <u>far</u>

1. _____
2. _____
3. _____
4. _____

/ir/ as in <u>ear</u>

9. _____
10. _____
11. _____
12. _____

/ôr/ as in <u>for</u>

5. _____
6. _____
7. _____
8. _____

/er/ as in <u>air</u>

13. _____
14. _____
15. _____

Sound-Spellings

Write the List Word for each sound-spelling given.
Use your dictionary if you need help.

In a dictionary, a **sound-spelling** appears after each entry word. It tells how to pronounce the word. **start** (stärt)

1. (ôr´ dər) _____

2. (bē fôr´) _____

3. (ker) _____

4. (yir) _____

5. (lärj) _____

6. (cher) _____

7. (klir) _____

8. (chir) _____

9. (pär´ tē) _____

10. (môrn´ iŋ) _____

11. (kəm per´) _____

12. (ə pir´) _____

Classification

Write the List Word that belongs in each group.

1. plant, flower, _____

2. knife, spoon, _____

3. day, month, _____

4. night, afternoon, _____

5. big, huge, _____

6. celebration, gathering, _____

7. yell, shout, _____

Flex Your Spelling Muscles

Writing

Imagine that you have been chosen to make a salad for the 200th birthday of your own town. What are you going to put in it? Write a recipe telling how to make your salad. Use as many List Words as you can.

Proofreading

Each sentence below has two mistakes. Use the proofreading marks to fix each mistake. Write the misspelled List Words on the lines.

Proofreading Marks	
⬭	spelling mistake
≡	capital letter

1. my mother planted a vegetable gardin last year.

1. _____

2. she asked me to help take kare of it.

2. _____

3. So I watered it befour school every mornin.

3. _____

_____

4. i made sure to keep the weeds cler.

4. _____

5. The vegetables grew very larje that yer.

5. _____

Now proofread your recipe. Fix any mistakes.

_____

Go for the Goal

Take your Final Test. Then fill in your Scoreboard. Send your mistakes to the Word Locker.

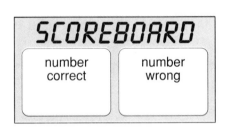

SCOREBOARD

number correct	number wrong

★ ★ ★ ★ ★ ★ ★ ★ ★ ★ **All-Star Words** ★ ★ ★ ★ ★ ★ ★ ★ ★ ★

darkness   fear   airport   harm   forward

Write each All-Star Word and a clue to go with it. Then get together with a partner. Can you guess the All-Star Word that goes with each clue?

Name _____

Vowels with r

Warm Up

Why do people come to the National Hollerin' Contest?

Give a Hoot

Every year on the **third Saturday** in June, folks gather to hoot and holler. The place is Spivey's Corner, North Carolina. The people come here to **honor** the past by yelling.

Years ago around these parts, you could hear hollering every day. **Early** in the morning on their way to work, farmers would holler to each other. **First,** one **farmer** would yell. Then another would take a turn. Several more would join in. Before long, people were hollerin' from miles away. Each farmer tried to yell **better** and louder than the last. Each one had a special style. Neighbors could recognize one another's yells. It was a signal that the work day was beginning, just like an early morning hello.

Today, there's no need to yell in Spivey's Corner. Now there are telephones! Once a year though, people still holler. The best and the loudest yellers come from all around. You could call Spivey's Corner the "hollerin' capital of the world." But don't say it too loud, it might **hurt** your ears.

Say the words in dark print in the selection. What vowel sound with **r** do you hear in each word?

On Your Mark

Take your Warm Up Test. Then check your spelling with the List Words on the next page.

Each List Word contains the /ʉr/ sound. It can be spelled many ways. Look at each List Word to see how the /ʉr/ sound is spelled:

first **lear**n **wor**k sug**ar** pap**er** h**ur**t
When the /ʉr/ sound is found in a syllable that is not accented, its sound-symbol is /ər/.

LIST WORDS

1. early   *early*
2. third   *third*
3. workbook   *workbook*
4. first   *first*
5. worry   *worry*
6. hurt   *hurt*
7. Saturday   *Saturday*
8. better   *better*
9. farmer   *farmer*
10. honor   *honor*
11. sugar   *sugar*
12. nurse   *nurse*
13. earth   *earth*
14. paper   *paper*
15. learn   *learn*

Game Plan

Spelling Lineup
Write each List Word under the correct spelling of the /ʉr/ sound.

ir

1. _____

2. _____

ur

3. _____

4. _____

5. _____

ear

6. _____

7. _____

8. _____

er

9. _____

10. _____

11. _____

or

12. _____

13. _____

14. _____

ar

15. _____

Dictionary

Write the List Words that would appear on a dictionary page that has the **guide words** below. Make sure the words are in alphabetical order.

In a dictionary, **guide words** at the top of a page show the first and last entries found on that page.
divide/first

eye/hunt

1. _____

2. _____

3. _____

out/sun

4. _____

5. _____

6. _____

Puzzle

Fill in the crossword puzzle by writing a List Word to answer each clue.

ACROSS
1. more excellent
8. to gain knowledge
9. There's no school today!
10. sweetener
11. high regard; fame

DOWN
2. after second
3. not late
4. book of school activities
5. the planet we live on
6. school supply
7. medical worker

Flex Your Spelling Muscles

Writing

Use the List Words to create a poster to advertise a contest you know about or would like to have. Remember to include important information such as what kind of contest it is, and when and where it will take place.

Proofreading

Each sentence below has two mistakes. Use the proofreading marks to fix each mistake. Write the misspelled List Words on the lines.

Proofreading Marks	
⬭	spelling mistake
⊙	add period

1. Many years ago, people in Africa used drums instead of papir to communicate

2. They could lurn about other people bettur and faster with drums.

3. The drums could tell if someone was hert and if a doctor was needed

4. The drums held a special place of honar among the people

1. _____

2. _____

   _____

3. _____

4. _____

Now proofread your poster.
Fix any mistakes.

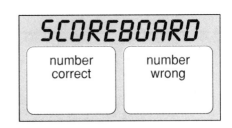

Go for the Goal

Take your Final Test. Then fill in your Scoreboard. Send your mistakes to the Word Locker.

SCOREBOARD

number correct	number wrong

★ ★ ★ ★ ★ ★ ★ ★ ★ **All-Star Words** ★ ★ ★ ★ ★ ★ ★ ★ ★

churn   earn   dessert   squirm   afford

Write a sentence for each word, then erase the All-Star Word. Trade papers with a partner. Write the word that belongs in each blank.

Name _____

Suffixes Added to Root Words

Warm Up

What, other than fire detection, can a lookout tower be used for?

Above the Crowds

If you're in the mood for a mountain vacation, and you don't care to go **camping,** why not try a week in a lookout tower? In many national forests across the country people are doing just that—vacationing in old fire lookout towers.

At one time the Forest Service relied heavily on these towers. From them rangers **studied** the forest for signs of forest fire. Today, the Forest Service depends mostly on airplanes that are much more efficient and can pinpoint the exact locations of fires. As a result, many of the older lookout towers are no longer being used. However, volunteers have begun taking an interest in saving these buildings. They have started **cleaning** and repairing towers that need repairs.

If you like fancy hotels, you may not like a lookout tower. Many are five stories high, and the bathrooms are on the ground. There is no electricity and you have to haul up your own water. And if you are **worried** about lightning, stay home. Lightning strikes are a pretty common event. Although the towers are fairly safe, a lightning bolt can be shocking! As one visitor said, "It's like being on the inside of a light bulb when someone turns it on."

Look back at the words in dark print. What do you notice about their spelling? Did the root words change when an ending, or suffix, was added?

On Your Mark

Take your Warm Up Test. Then check your spelling with the List Words on the next page.

Pep Talk

A **suffix** is added at the end of a **root word.** If a word ends in a vowel and **y,** add only the suffix—**stay** + **ed** = stayed. If a word ends in a consonant and **y,** change the **y** to **i** before adding the suffix unless the suffix begins with **i.**

worry + **ed** = worried

worry + **ing** = worrying

LIST WORDS

1. rained   *rained*
2. prayed   *prayed*
3. studied   *studied*
4. cleaning   *cleaning*
5. thanked   *thanked*
6. acted   *acted*
7. worried   *worried*
8. helped   *helped*
9. copying   *copying*
10. flying   *flying*
11. hurried   *hurried*
12. married   *married*
13. dressing   *dressing*
14. camping   *camping*
15. replied   *replied*

Game Plan

Spelling Lineup

Write the List Words. In some List Words, you must change the **y** to **i.**

1. rain + ed = _____

2. pray + ed = _____

3. study + ed = _____

4. clean + ing = _____

5. thank + ed = _____

6. act + ed = _____

7. worry + ed = _____

8. help + ed = _____

9. copy + ing = _____

10. fly + ing = _____

11. hurry + ed = _____

12. marry + ed = _____

13. dress + ing = _____

14. camp + ing = _____

15. reply + ed = _____

Classification

Write the List Word that belongs in each group.

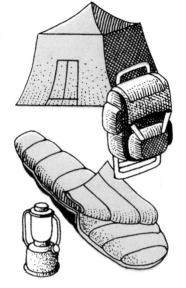

1. school, tests, books, _____

2. tent, sleeping bag, backpack, _____

3. bride, groom, ring, _____

4. stage, play, theater, _____

5. clouds, lightning, thunder, _____

6. said, answered, responded, _____

7. soap, water, dirt, _____

8. shirt, pants, jacket, _____

Missing Words

Add **ing** or **ed** to a root word from the box to make List Words.
Write a List Word to finish each sentence.

help	fly	copy	thank
study	hurry	worry	pray

1. I _____ my grandparents for the gift.

2. David _____ his dad do the housework.

3. I am _____ the words onto my paper now.

4. The farmers _____ for rain.

5. My parents were _____ when I came home late from school.

6. I _____ to reach the store before it closed.

7. The pilot is _____ around the world.

8. Paul and I _____ together in the library.

Flex Your Spelling Muscles

Writing

Have you ever been on a camping trip, or wondered what it would be like? Write a story about a camping trip you've taken or would like to take. Use as many List Words as you can.

Proofreading

Each sentence below has two mistakes. Use the proofreading marks to fix each mistake. Write the misspelled List Words on the lines.

Proofreading Marks	
⬭	spelling mistake
⊙	add period

1. Teddy Roosevelt was a president who studyed the environment

2. He wooried about what was happening to the wild lands in our country

3. He helpet save the forests and wildlife

4. Most people tainked him for what he did

1. _____

2. _____

3. _____

4. _____

Now proofread your story. Fix any mistakes.

Go for the Goal

Take your Final Test. Then fill in your Scoreboard. Send your mistakes to the Word Locker.

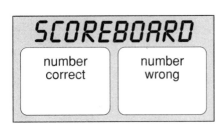

SCOREBOARD

number correct	number wrong

★ ★ ★ ★ ★ ★ ★ ★ **All-Star Words** ★ ★ ★ ★ ★ ★ ★ ★

tossed   scolding   frying   satisfied   spied

Write a sentence using each All-Star Word, but erase the word's suffix. Trade papers with a partner. Finish each other's sentences.

Name _____

Suffixes Added to Root Words

Warm Up

Why would people call Mark Spitz the best swimmer in the world?

Golden Boy

Mark Spitz won nine Olympic gold medals in the 1968 and 1972 Olympic games. That means he came in first in nine races. He also won a silver medal for second place and a bronze medal for third place in two other races. With eleven Olympic medals, Mark Spitz became the most famous **swimmer** in the world and the **biggest** winner of Olympic medals.

At age six Mark was just **beginning** swimming lessons. By the time he was ten, he was known for **setting** a record. It was in the 50-yard race for nine- and ten-year-olds. He won that race in less time than anyone in that age group had ever done before.

To this day, no one has ever won as many Olympic medals as Mark Spitz. But when that day finally comes, it'll really be something to see!

Look back at the words in dark print. What do you notice about the spelling of the root words when the suffixes are added?

On Your Mark

Take your Warm Up Test. Then check your spelling with the List Words on the next page.

65

LIST WORDS

1. swimmer *swimmer*
2. biggest *biggest*
3. winner *winner*
4. cutting *cutting*
5. foggy *foggy*
6. setting *setting*
7. stopped *stopped*
8. wetter *wetter*
9. slipped *slipped*
10. stepping *stepping*
11. beginning *beginning*
12. admitted *admitted*
13. jogger *jogger*
14. flexing *flexing*
15. waxed *waxed*

Game Plan

Spelling Lineup

Write each List Word whose final consonant was doubled before the suffix was added. Circle each suffix.

1. _____ 8. _____

2. _____ 9. _____

3. _____ 10. _____

4. _____ 11. _____

5. _____ 12. _____

6. _____ 13. _____

7. _____

Write each List Word that did not have the final consonant doubled before the suffix was added. Circle each suffix.

14. _____ 15. _____

Rhyming

Write the List Word that rhymes with each word given.

1. netting _____

2. taxed _____

3. letter _____

4. clipped _____

5. logger _____

6. chopped _____

Definitions

Write the List Word that matches the meaning given. Then read down the shaded boxes to answer the riddle.

1. largest

2. misty and cloudy

3. said to be true

4. dividing into parts

5. one who moves in water

6. walking

7. polished

8. bending or tightening your muscles

Riddle: What does a boat eat for breakfast?

Answer: _____

Flex Your Spelling Muscles

Writing

What is your favorite sport? Write a few sentences naming the sport you like best and why. Use as many List Words as you can.

Proofreading

Each sentence below has two mistakes. Use the proofreading marks to fix each mistake. Write the misspelled List Words on the lines.

Proofreading Marks	
⬭	spelling mistake
≡	capital letter
⊙	add period

1. In the beegining, the Olympic games were held in greece.

1. _____

2. today, the seting of the Olympics changes each time they are held.

2. _____

3. Some cities have never stopt wanting to host the games

3. _____

4. Maybe one day your town will have the top swimar in the Olympics

4. _____

Now proofread your sentences about sports. Fix any mistakes.

Goal for the Goal

Take your Final Test. Then fill in your Scoreboard. Send your mistakes to the Word Locker.

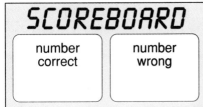

SCOREBOARD

number correct	number wrong

★ ★ ★ ★ ★ ★ ★ ★ All-Star Words ★ ★ ★ ★ ★ ★ ★ ★

stirred   dimmer   clapping   smoggy   maddest

Write a sentence for each All-Star Word. Trade papers with a partner. Circle the suffix in the All-Star Word in each sentence.

Suffixes Added to Root Words

Warm Up

Can cars really use sunlight as fuel?

Racing on Sunshine

In an unusual event called Sunrayce, a car that looked like a pizza box **chased** another car that looked like a torpedo on wheels. **Racing** up from behind was still another car that looked like a huge telephone handle. These cars had one thing in common—they were all solar-powered. Each car had dark, shiny photoelectric cells that sparkled in the sunlight—a **lovely** and energy-saving sight!

These cars were built by science and engineering students from thirty-two American and Canadian colleges. The idea of the race was for each team to turn sunlight into enough electrical power to drive a car about 1,600 miles. Because the motors were electric, the only thing **noisy** was the crowd of people watching!

Car manufacturers are **making** great progress with electric cars. However, it is unlikely that we will use solar-powered cars in our everyday lives. A solar car would have to carry enough battery power so that the car could run even when the sun isn't shining.

Events like Sunrayce give scientists a chance to study new ideas that could be put to use one day in the future.

Look back at the boldfaced words in the selection. Name the root words. Which words changed their spelling when an **ed, ing, y,** or **ly** was added?

On Your Mark

Take your Warm Up Test. Then check your spelling with the List Words on the next page.

If a word ends in a silent **e,** drop the **e** before adding a suffix that begins with a vowel.

chase + **ed** = chased

make + **ing** = making

In some words ending with silent **e,** drop the **e** before adding **y.**

ice + **y** = icy

Keep the final **e** when adding the suffix **ly.**

nice + **ly** = nicely

LIST WORDS

1. chased *chased*
2. shared *shared*
3. taking *taking*
4. living *living*
5. making *making*
6. noisy *noisy*
7. icy *icy*
8. racing *racing*
9. dancing *dancing*
10. nicely *nicely*
11. lovely *lovely*
12. closely *closely*
13. lately *lately*
14. framed *framed*
15. hoped *hoped*

Game Plan

Spelling Lineup

Write the List Words under the correct heading. Circle the suffixes.

words with **ing** that tell about present action

1. _____   4. _____

2. _____   5. _____

3. _____

words that tell about past action

6. _____   8. _____

7. _____   9. _____

words that end with the suffix **y**

10. _____   11. _____

words that end with the suffix **ly**

12. _____   14. _____

13. _____   15. _____

Suffixes

Make a List Word from the root in each sentence. Circle the root word and add a suffix from the box. Write the List Words.

ed   ing   ly   y

1. The road was ice. _____

2. Maria has a love voice. _____

3. Mom and Dad watched the road close. _____

4. Dan nice offered to set the table. _____

5. Tom share his piece of carrot cake with me. _____

6. The loud music was make my head hurt. _____

7. Aunt Josie is live in a new city. _____

8. Kim and Jo are race to catch the school bus. _____

9. We hope that Dad would win the contest, but _____ he lost.

10. Pat is dance in our school play. _____

Scrambled Letters

Unscramble the letters to spell List Words. Write the List Words.

1. mardef _____

2. shcade _____

3. gatkin _____

4. teally _____

5. inyso _____

6. cosylle _____

Flex Your Spelling Muscles

Writing

Would you like to invent a new kind of transportation? Draw a picture of your invention. Write a brief description of it. Use as many List Words as you can.

Proofreading

This paragraph has nine mistakes. Use the proofreading marks to fix each mistake. Write the misspelled List Words on the lines.

Proofreading Marks
⬭ spelling mistake
∧ add something
≡ capital letter

Do you like looking clozely at old cars If you do, there is a lovily festival you can go to at the Henry Ford Museum in dearborn, Michigan. In august, you can see old rasing cars from the 1950s. Perhaps their owners will let you listen to the noizy engines! Will you be one of the visitors takeng lots of pictures

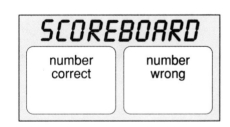

1. _____   3. _____   5. _____

2. _____   4. _____

Now proofread your description. Fix any mistakes.

Go for the Goal

Take your Final Test. Then fill in your Scoreboard. Send your mistakes to the Word Locker.

SCOREBOARD

number correct	number wrong

★ ★ ★ ★ ★ ★ ★ ★ ★   All-Star Words   ★ ★ ★ ★ ★ ★ ★ ★ ★

losing   gazed   spicy   politely   serving

Write each All-Star Word. Then write a clue to go with it. Read each clue aloud to a partner. Ask your partner for the All-Star Word that goes with the clue.

Instant Replay • Lessons 13–17

Time Out

Take another look at vowels with **r** and suffixes added to root words.

Check Your Word Locker

Look at the words in your Word Locker. Which words for Lessons 13 through 17 did you have the most trouble with? Write them here.

_____

_____

Practice writing your troublesome words with a partner. Take turns spelling the words aloud while your partner writes the words on the board.

Lesson 13

The letter **r** can change the sound of a vowel in a word. Listen for the vowel sounds in party, fork, year, and care.

List Words
large
start
before
morning
clear
appear

Write a List Word that means the opposite of each word given.

1. after _____

2. small _____

3. vanish _____

4. finish _____

5. muddy _____

6. evening _____

73

The /ʉr/ sound you hear in <u>hurt</u> can be spelled with **ir, or, er, ear, ar,** or **ur.** When the /ʉr/ sound is found in a syllable that is not accented, its sound-symbol is /ər/.

List Words

early
fish
honor
sugar
earth
learn

Write each List Word under the number of syllables it contains.

one syllable   **two syllables**

1. _____   4. _____

2. _____   5. _____

3. _____   6. _____

Root words often change their spelling when a suffix is added. For a word ending with a vowel and **y,** add only the suffix, as in <u>prayed</u>. For a word ending with a consonant and **y,** change the **y** to **i** before adding the suffix unless the suffix begins with **i,** as in <u>married</u> and <u>marrying</u>.

List Words

rained
studied
worried
copying
hurried
replied

Write a List Word that matches each clue.

1. went faster   _____

2. answered the question   _____

3. made the day wet   _____

4. did schoolwork   _____

5. doing the same thing again   _____

6. bothered   _____

For short-vowel words that end with one consonant other than **y,** double the consonant before adding a suffix that begins with a vowel, as in <u>stopped</u> and <u>cutting</u>.

List Words

swimmer
biggest
winner
slipped
beginning
admitted

Write this set of List Words in alphabetical order. Draw a circle around each root word.

1. _____

2. _____

3. _____

4. _____

5. _____

6. _____

Lesson 17

For words that end with a silent **e,** drop the **e** when you add a suffix that begins with a vowel, as in <u>framed</u>. Keep the final **e** when adding **ly,** as in <u>lately</u>.

List Words

living
noisy
icy
nicely
lovely
hoped

Write the List Word that means the same or almost the same as each word given.

1. frozen _____

2. wished _____

3. kindly _____

4. alive _____

5. beautiful _____

6. loud _____

List Words

admitted
honor
studied
sugar
copying
start
icy
large

Fill in the crossword puzzle by writing a List Word to answer each clue.

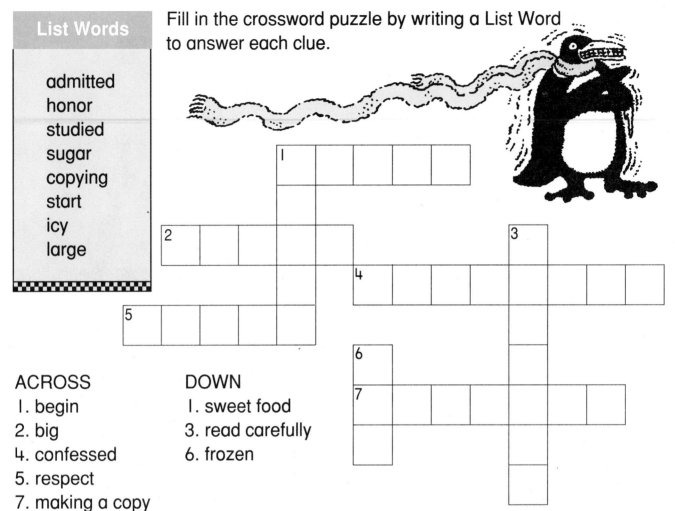

ACROSS
1. begin
2. big
4. confessed
5. respect
7. making a copy

DOWN
1. sweet food
3. read carefully
6. frozen

Go for the Goal

Take your Final Replay Test. Then fill in your Scoreboard. Send any misspelled words to your Word Locker.

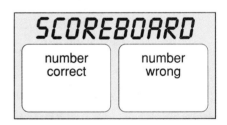

SCOREBOARD

number correct	number wrong

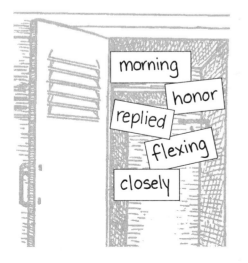

morning
honor
replied
flexing
closely

Clean Out Your Word Locker

Look in your Word Locker. Cross out each word you spelled correctly on your Final Replay Test. Circle the words you're still having trouble with. Add the words you circled to your Spelling Notebook. What do you notice about the words? Watch for those words as you write.

Name _____

Regular Plurals: Adding s or es

Warm Up

What are these hunters gathering?

Hide and Seek

It is early fall in the forests of Oregon and Washington. For six weeks every year, armies of cone **hunters** search the woods here. They look for **cones** with plenty of seeds. Lumber and seed companies pay them for the best cones. The seeds are then used to plant new forests around the world.

The best cones are hard to find. They grow on **branches** high in the trees. The hunters don't need to climb the trees to get the cones. They just let the squirrels do the job. Then they find the places where the squirrels hide them. To do this, a good hunter must think like a squirrel.

Are the hunters stealing food from squirrels? "The squirrels will never go hungry," says one cone hunter. "They are too clever. We never find all their hiding places. We might be just a few **inches** away from one place and not find it. If I thought I was starving a squirrel, I'd bring the squirrel some nuts and trade them for the cones. Squirrels also eat **berries** and nuts. We may be taking some pine cones, but we're giving the squirrels more trees in the years to come."

Look back at the words in dark print. They are all nouns that name more than one. What do you notice about their spelling?

On Your Mark

Take your Warm Up Test. Then check your spelling with the List Words on the next page.

Pep Talk

Singular nouns name one person, place, or thing. Plural nouns name more than one. Add **s** to most singular nouns to make them plural.

If a noun ends in **x, s, sh,** or **ch,** add **es** to make it plural. If a noun ends with a consonant and **y,** change the **y** to **i** and add **es.**

LIST WORDS

1. cones
2. hunters
3. desks
4. babies
5. berries
6. puppies
7. bushes
8. bunches
9. brushes
10. branches
11. inches
12. taxes
13. classes
14. dishes
15. watches

Game Plan

Spelling Lineup

Write each List Word under the correct heading. The heading tells what to do to a singular word to form the plural List Word.

add **s**

1. _____
2. _____
3. _____

change **y** to **i,**
and add **es**

4. _____
5. _____
6. _____

add **es**

7. _____
8. _____
9. _____
10. _____
11. _____
12. _____
13. _____
14. _____
15. _____

Rhyming

Write List Words that rhyme with the words given.

1. phones _____

2. rushes _____

3. guppies _____

4. waxes _____

5. glasses _____

6. ferries _____

7. pinches _____

8. wishes _____

Scrambled Letters Puzzle

Unscramble the letters to spell List Words. Print one letter in each box. Then read down the shaded boxes to answer the riddle.

1. EREBRIS

2. SEATX

3. SERNBACH

4. SIABBE

5. CINSHE

6. AHETWCS

7. SKEDS

8. SIUPPEP

9. UNTRESH

Riddle: Why does the Statue of Liberty stand in New York Harbor?

Answer: ___ ___   ___ ___ ___ '   ___ ___ ___ .

Flex Your Spelling Muscles

Writing

Have you ever watched a squirrel or other wild animal?
Write a description about what you saw. Use as many
List Words as you can.

Proofreading

This article about squirrels has eight mistakes. Use the
proofreading marks to fix the mistakes. Then write the
misspelled List Words on the lines.

Proofreading Marks
⬭ spelling mistake
◞ take out something

Baby squirrels hide in tree branchs until they
feel brave enough to to climb down. The mother
wachis over them as they explore. She shows
them in which bushs tasty buntchas of beries can
be found and how to gather coans for the winter.
If danger is is near, the mother squirrel bravely
drives off the enemy to protect her young.

1. _____

2. _____

3. _____

4. _____

5. _____

6. _____

Now proofread your description. Fix any mistakes.

Go for the Goal

Take your Final Test. Then fill in your Scoreboard.
Send your mistakes to the Word Locker.

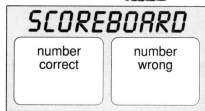

SCOREBOARD

number correct	number wrong

★ ★ ★ ★ ★ ★ ★ ★ ★ **All-Star Words** ★ ★ ★ ★ ★ ★ ★ ★ ★

sweaters   butterflies   polishes   businesses   mixes

Write a sentence for each word. Swap papers with your partner.
Circle the plural endings of the All-Star Words.

Irregular Plurals

Warm Up

What did Rant Mullens use to make Bigfoot's "footprints"?

Trick Feet

In the state of Washington, folks tell about a giant monster. It's called Bigfoot of Mount Saint Helens. Over the years, its giant footprints have been seen by **men, women,** and **children.** Stories about the scary monster are still told everywhere.

A few years ago, Rant Mullens claimed to know the truth about Bigfoot. He said he started it himself as a joke in 1928. Using some **knives** and other tools, he cut two huge feet out of wood. Then he used the wooden feet to make the big footprints. Mr. Mullens explained that there is no real Bigfoot. It seems his joke may have fooled a lot of people for almost sixty years!

The joke may be on Mr. Mullens himself. By creating fake tracks, Mr. Mullens encouraged research into the possibility of a real Bigfoot. A scientist named Dr. Krantz studied many Bigfoot stories and tracks. He said the footprints made by Rant Mullens didn't match other Bigfoot tracks. Before Mr. Mullens told his story, scientists couldn't figure that out. In fact, Mr. Mullens' story may help to prove that perhaps a Bigfoot really does exist.

Look back at the words in dark print. All the words are plural nouns. What is the singular form of each word?

On Your Mark

Take your Warm Up Test. Then check your spelling with the List Words on the next page.

Singular nouns ending with **f** or **fe** often form plurals by changing the **f** or **fe** to **v** and adding **es.**
Some nouns have irregular plurals that do not end with **s.** Irregular plurals change their spelling or stay the same.

LIST WORDS

1. men
2. women
3. children
4. loaves
5. teeth
6. mice
7. deer
8. sheep
9. lives
10. fish
11. leaves
12. knives
13. wolves
14. oxen
15. wives
16. heroes
17. potatoes
18. geese
19. shelves
20. cattle

Game Plan

Spelling Lineup

Write the List Words that do not end with **s.**

1. _____   7. _____

2. _____   8. _____

3. _____   9. _____

4. _____   10. _____

5. _____   11. _____

6. _____

Write the List Words that have singular forms that end with **f** or **fe.**

12. _____   16. _____

13. _____   17. _____

14. _____   18. _____

15. _____

Write the List Words that have singular forms that end with the letter **o.**

19. _____   20. _____

Word Building

Build List Words by adding and subtracting letters. Write the List Words.

1. deal – al + er _____

2. worn – rn + men _____

3. shell – l + ves _____

4. tomatoes – tom + pot _____

5. loan – n + ves _____

6. twice – tw + m _____

7. with – wi + tee _____

8. lives – l + w _____

9. little – li + ca _____

10. lift – ft + ves _____

Word Puzzle

Write the List Word that matches each clue given.
Then read down the shaded boxes to answer the riddle.
Here's what they can do . . .

1. swim

2. say "baa"

3. fall off trees

4. run fast

5. grow up

6. cut

7. be dads

8. fly

9. do brave deeds

10. howl at the moon

11. pull heavy carts

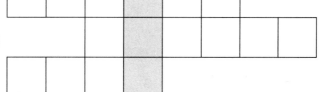

Riddle: What should you do if you meet a hungry monster?

Answer: _____ _____ _____ .

Flex Your Spelling Muscles

Writing

Finding a real Bigfoot would be an amazing story. Use the List Words to write a make-believe newspaper story telling about your discovery of Bigfoot.

Proofreading

This informational story has nine mistakes. Use the proofreading marks to fix the mistakes. Then write the misspelled List Words on the lines.

Proofreading Marks

◯ spelling mistake

^ add something

/ make small letter

In some parts of Asia, man, women, and childrun talk about the yeti, or the abominable snowman. The yeti supposedly livz in the high mountains. Those who claim to have seen it say that it is big and covered with hair like an Ape. What a sight It would be to see one! Some people think The yeti may just be large woolvs or some other animals that eat catel. What do you think

1. _____

2. _____

3. _____

4. _____

5. _____

Now proofread your newspaper story. Fix any mistakes.

Go for the Goal

Take your Final Test. Then fill in your Scoreboard. Send your mistakes to the Word Locker.

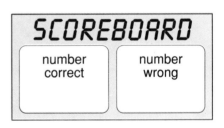

SCOREBOARD

| number correct | number wrong |

★ ★ ★ ★ ★ ★ ★ ★ ★ **All-Star Words** ★ ★ ★ ★ ★ ★ ★ ★ ★

bison   halves   scarves   buffaloes   thieves

Work with a partner to write a story, using each word. Then erase the All-Star Words. Trade stories with other students. Write the All-Star Words in the story.

Vowel Pairs

Warm Up

What are many people afraid of?

Speak Up!

What happens when the **teacher** calls on you? Do your mouth and throat get dry? Do you start to shake and forget everything you know? If so, you are not alone. Many people feel the same way.

Some scientists asked people what things made them afraid. Some people **said** they were afraid of bugs. Others said they were afraid of being in high places. Many people said they were afraid to **speak** in front of a **group** of people.

Is this true for you? Is speaking in front of your class one of your great fears? You don't have to be afraid. Here are some tips that will help you:

1. Be prepared. If you are **ready,** you will know what to say or have a good answer.
2. Be proud. You have something important to say.
3. Remember that you are not alone. Sooner or later, everyone gets called on. Your classmates don't want you to **fail,** because they don't want to fail either.
4. Last, but not least, speak up. Talk in a loud and clear voice.

 Say each word in dark print in the selection. Each word has two vowels that come together. What sounds do the vowel pairs make in the words?

On Your Mark

Take your Warm Up Test. Then check your spelling with the List Words on the next page.

In a vowel pair, the first vowel usually stands for a long sound and the second vowel is silent.   teacher = /ē/   fail = /ā/
Some words do not follow this rule.
group = /o͞o/
Vowel pairs may also have a short sound.
said = /e/   ready = /e/

LIST WORDS

1. teacher
2. feel
3. speak
4. clue
5. fail
6. soak
7. below
8. lie
9. needle
10. said
11. group
12. feast
13. ready
14. cheap
15. again
16. throat
17. eager
18. sooner
19. least
20. contain

Game Plan

Spelling Lineup

Write each List Word under the correct heading.
One word is used twice.

/ā/ as in <u>day</u>

1. _____
2. _____

/ē/ as in <u>meet</u>

3. _____
4. _____
5. _____
6. _____
7. _____
8. _____
9. _____
10. _____
11. _____

/ī/ as in <u>mile</u>

12. _____

/o/ as in <u>home</u>

13. _____
14. _____
15. _____

/e/ as in <u>red</u>

16. _____
17. _____
18. _____

/o͞o/ as in <u>tool</u>

19. _____
20. _____
21. _____

Classification

Write the List Word that belongs in each group.

1. touch, taste, _____

2. anxious, willing, _____

3. spoke, talked, _____

4. wash, scrub, _____

5. hint, suggestion, _____

6. sit, stand, _____

7. neck, mouth, _____

8. crowd, gang, _____

Syllables

Write each two-syllable List Word.

1. _____

2. _____

3. _____

4. _____

5. _____

6. _____

7. _____

8. _____

Definitions

Write the List Word that matches the meaning given. Use the number code to answer the riddle. Find the letter with the number 1 under it. Put that letter on each line below with the number 1 under it. Do the same for numbers 2 through 8.

1. a person who works at a school ___ ___ ___ ___ ___ ___ ___
                                                8   1   2

2. not to win or succeed ___ ___ ___ ___
                          6

3. smallest in size or amount ___ ___ ___ ___ ___
                              3   4

4. to say, tell, whisper, or shout ___ ___ ___ ___ ___
                              7   5

Riddle: What did the goat have when it ate the dollar bill?

Answer: It had a ___ ___ ___ ___ ___   ___ ___ ___ ___ ___ !
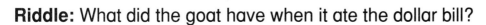
            1 2 3 4 5   6 3 4 7 8

Flex Your Spelling Muscles

Writing

Have you ever had to give a book report, read, or speak in front of a group of people? How did it make you feel? Use the List Words to write a paragraph sharing your feelings.

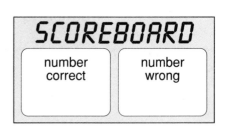

Proofreading

The diary entry below has ten mistakes. Use the proofreading marks to fix the mistakes. Write the misspelled List Words on the lines.

Proofreading Marks
⬯ spelling mistake
≡ capital letter
⚲ take out something

september 12, 1993

    Am I glad this day is over! today my teecher asked me to speke in front of the class. When she called my name, I started to fele nervous. Then my my throet felt like it was closing up and my legs started to shake. Finally, I sed to myself, "The souner I get started, the sooner I'll be done." Now that it's all over, I'm not not quite sure why I was so nervous—it really wasn't too bad.

1. _____

2. _____

3. _____

4. _____

5. _____

6. _____

Now proofread your paragraph. Fix any mistakes.

Go for the Goal

Take your Final Test. Then fill in your Scoreboard. Send your mistakes to the Word Locker.

SCOREBOARD

number correct	number wrong

★ ★ ★ ★ ★ ★ ★ ★ **All-Star Words** ★ ★ ★ ★ ★ ★ ★ ★ ★

bouquet   beneath   steady   stain   mood

Try to use all five All-Star Words in a single sentence. Then get together with a partner and compare sentences.

Double o

Warm Up

What does Slip! Slop! Slap! mean?

Save Your Skin!

Did you know that the sun can damage your skin? The sun's ultraviolet rays cause sunburn, which can harm, dry, and age your skin. But, if you follow these safety tips, you won't have to say **goodbye** to the sun.

- Avoid direct sunlight, especially at midday. The sun is the hottest in the late morning or early **afternoon.** It doesn't mean that you have to stay away from the beach or **pool.** Just stay in a shady spot. It's **cooler** in the shade!
- Bring an umbrella, or wear a big hat.
- Use sunscreen. **Choose** one that has a high SPF. *SPF* means sunburn protection factor. A SPF of 30 protects the skin 30 times longer than with no protection at all.
- If you do get burned, **soothe** the ache with aloe cream.

Even in Australia, where there is so much sunny weather, people are beginning to pay attention to the warnings, especially lifeguards. At the beach, they always try to sit in shaded areas and wear t-shirts that read Slip! Slop! Slap! Almost everybody "Down Under" understands that to mean, "Slip on a shirt. Slop on some sunscreen. Slap on a hat!"

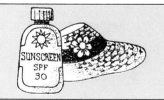

Look back at the words in dark print. Notice that each word has the vowel pair **oo.** Say each word. How many different vowel sounds do you hear?

On Your Mark

Take your Warm Up Test. Then check your spelling with the List Words on the next page.

Pep Talk

The vowel pair **oo** stands for three sounds.
/ōō/ as in <u>cooler</u>   /ōo/ as in <u>brook</u>
/u/ as in <u>blood</u>
Listen for the sound the vowel pair **oo** stands for in each List Word.

LIST WORDS

1. scoop
2. shoot
3. afternoon
4. cooler
5. roof
6. broom
7. pool
8. choose
9. goose
10. soothe
11. loose
12. stood
13. goodness
14. wool
15. brook
16. cookie
17. goodbye
18. wooden
19. soot
20. blood

Game Plan

Spelling Lineup

Write each List Word under the correct heading.

/ōō/ as in <u>cool</u>

1. _____
2. _____
3. _____
4. _____
5. _____
6. _____
7. _____
8. _____
9. _____
10. _____
11. _____

/ōo/ as in <u>book</u>

12. _____
13. _____
14. _____
15. _____
16. _____
17. _____
18. _____
19. _____

/u/ as in <u>flood</u>

20. _____

Alphabetical Order

Write each group of List Words in alphabetical order.

pool	soothe	wooden
shoot	stood	wool

1. _____

2. _____

3. _____

4. _____

5. _____

6. _____

brook	blood	goose
goodness	cooler	cookie

7. _____

8. _____

9. _____

10. _____

11. _____

12. _____

Comparing Words

Read the first two underlined words in each sentence. Write the List Word that goes with the third word in the same way.

1. Come is to leave as hello is to _____ .

2. Night is to day as evening is to _____ .

3. Snow is to shovel as dust is to _____ .

4. Head is to hat as building is to _____ .

5. Fireplace is to ash as chimney is to _____ .

Flex Your Spelling Muscles

Writing

The danger of ultraviolet rays makes sunscreen important for everyone. Use the List Words to write a persuasive ad that will convince people to use sunscreen.

Proofreading

The recipe below has nine mistakes. Use the proofreading marks to fix the mistakes. Then write the misspelled List Words on the lines.

Summer Salad

Here's a recipe that will make a warm summer afternun just a little bit couler.

- First, chooz your favorite kinds of melons. watermelon, Honeydew, and cantaloupe are the best.
- next, cut them in half and scoope out the insides using a melon baller.
- Then, use the Hollowed out skin of one of the melons as a bowl for the melon balls.
- finally, enjoy!

Proofreading Marks

⬭   spelling mistake

≡   capital letter

/   make small letter

1. _____

2. _____

3. _____

4. _____

Now proofread your sunscreen ad. Fix any mistakes.

Go for the Goal

Take your Final Test. Then fill in your Scoreboard. Send your mistakes to the Word Locker.

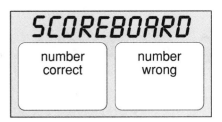

SCOREBOARD

number correct	number wrong

★ ★ ★ ★ ★ ★ ★ ★ ★ **All-Star Words** ★ ★ ★ ★ ★ ★ ★ ★ ★

bamboo   flood   raccoon   crooked   gloomy

Draw a picture to give a clue for each All-Star Word. Trade drawings with a partner. Can you write a caption for each picture using the correct All-Star Word?

Silent Consonants

Warm Up

What were the Pillars of Hercules?

Sign of the Times

What does this dollar sign look like? It looks something like a figure **eight.** That's because long ago, in the days of pirates, an eight was printed on Spanish coins called "pieces of eight." Each of these coins could be cut into eight pieces. One or more pieces could be used when something cost less money.

Why do two lines cut the eight in **half?** These lines stand for two high rocks at the southern tip of Spain. A long, long time ago, people told a story about a strong man named Hercules. They **thought** he might have split a big mountain in two with his bare hands. They claimed this opened a doorway to the Mediterranean Sea from the Atlantic Ocean. The two high rocks on either side of the doorway came to be called the Pillars of Hercules. Spanish sailors **would** often pass **through** the Pillars of Hercules. Therefore, the two lines were added to the sign to mark the coins as Spanish money.

Soon the $ came to mean dollar. And, of course, that's what it still means today.

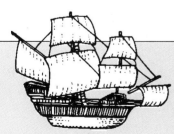

Say each word in dark print in the selection.
Which letters do not make a sound?

On Your Mark

Take your Warm Up Test. Then check your spelling with the List Words on the next page.

Pep Talk

In each List Word you will find that **gh** or **I** is not heard. Look for these spelling patterns in your List Words:

al is /a/ as in <u>calf</u>
igh is /ī/ as in <u>light</u>
oul is /oo/ as <u>would</u>
eigh is /ā/ as in <u>eight</u>
ough is /o͞o/ as in <u>through</u>
ough is /ô/ as in <u>fought</u>

LIST WORDS

1. fight
2. half
3. sight
4. would
5. night
6. light
7. calf
8. might
9. highway
10. moonlight
11. bright
12. eight
13. thought
14. through
15. weight
16. fright
17. sigh
18. slight
19. fought
20. knight

Game Plan

Spelling Lineup

Write each List Word under the correct heading. Circle the silent consonant or consonants in each word.

igh spells /ī/

1. _____
2. _____
3. _____
4. _____
5. _____
6. _____
7. _____
8. _____
9. _____
10. _____
11. _____
12. _____

al spells /a/

13. _____
14. _____

oul spells /oo/

15. _____

eigh spells /ā/

16. _____
17. _____

ough spells /o͞o/

18. _____

ough spells /ô/

19. _____
20. _____

Dictionary

Write the List Word for each sound-spelling given.

In a dictionary, a **sound-spelling** appears after each entry word. It tells how to pronounce the word. **weight** (wāt)

1. (fôt) _____

2. (slīt) _____

3. (brīt) _____

4. (wood) _____

5. (mīt) _____

6. (fīt) _____

7. (haf) _____

8. (āt) _____

9. (frīt) _____

10. (moon´ līt) _____

Homonyms

Words that sound alike but are spelled differently are called **homonyms.** Write the two List Words that are homonyms.

1. _____   2. _____

Puzzle

Fill in the crossword puzzle.

ACROSS
2. an idea
4. to let out a long, deep breath
7. a battle
8. main road

DOWN
1. in one side and out the other
3. how heavy something is
5. a lamp
6. a baby cow

Flex Your Spelling Muscles

Writing

Can you think of a different symbol that might be used to represent the dollar? Draw your idea. Then use the List Words to write a paragraph explaining why you chose your symbol.

Proofreading

This article has ten mistakes. Use the proofreading marks to fix each mistake. Write the misspelled List Words on the lines.

> The United states haff dollar is worth 50 cents. This brite silver-and-copper coin was first made in February of 1964 In 1975, the government thaut it woode be a good idea to issue a special half dollar for our country's 200th birthday This special coin, which showed independence Hall on one side, was made from 1975 thruw 1976. Although hard to find, half dollars are still being used today

Now proofread your paragraph. Fix any mistakes.

Proofreading Marks

⬭	spelling mistake
≡	capital letter
⊙	add period

1. _____

2. _____

3. _____

4. _____

5. _____

Go for the Goal

Take your Final Test. Then fill in your Scoreboard. Send your mistakes to the Word Locker.

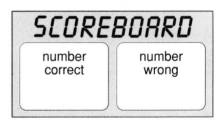

★ ★ ★ ★ ★ ★ ★ ★ ★ **All-Star Words** ★ ★ ★ ★ ★ ★ ★ ★ ★

flight   behalf   freight   although   sought

Write a sentence for each word, but leave a blank where the All-Star Word should be. Trade sentences with your partner. Write the correct words in the blanks.

Name _____

Instant Replay • Lessons 19–23

Time Out

Take another look at plurals, vowel pairs, and words with silent letters.

Check Your Word Locker

Look back at the words in your Word Locker.
Write your troublesome words for Lessons 19–23.

_____

_____

Practice writing your troublesome words with a partner. Form the letters of each word using clay. Your partner can spell the words aloud as you form the letters.

Lesson 19

Add **s** to most nouns to make them plural, as in <u>hunters</u>. If a noun ends in **x, s, sh,** or **ch,** add **es** to make it plural, as in <u>bunches</u>. If a noun ends in a consonant and **y,** change the **y** to **i** and add **es,** as in <u>berries</u>.

List Words
inches
desks
watches
bushes
puppies
babies

Write the List Words in alphabetical order.

1. _____   4. _____

2. _____   5. _____

3. _____   6. _____

If a word ends in **f** or **fe,** usually change the **f** or **fe** to **v** and add **es,** as in leaves. Some words change their vowel sound or spelling to make the plural form, as in men. Others have the same form for singular and plural, as in deer.

List Words
children
geese
sheep
wolves
heroes
women

Write each List Word under the correct heading.

animals

1. _____

2. _____

3. _____

people

4. _____

5. _____

6. _____

Most vowel pairs spell long-vowel sounds, as in least. A few words, such as said, do not follow this rule. Some vowel pairs spell short-vowel sounds, as in again.

List Words
group
soak
clue
speak
said
least

Write a List Word that rhymes with each word given.

1. fed _____

2. peek _____

3. feast _____

4. poke _____

5. loop _____

6. flew _____

The vowel pair **oo** can stand for three sounds, as in <u>scoop</u>, <u>soot</u>, and <u>blood</u>.

List Words

shoot
brook
choose
stood
cookie
soothe

Write each List Word under the word with the same vowel sound.

scoop

1. _____
2. _____
3. _____

good

4. _____
5. _____
6. _____

Some words contain silent letters, as in <u>half</u> and <u>sight</u>.

List Words

fight
calf
eight
would
highway
fright

Write the List Word that matches each clue.

1. a number _____

2. argue _____

3. a kind of road _____

4. sounds like <u>wood</u> _____

5. feeling of fear _____

6. baby cow _____

Lesson 24 ■ Instant Replay   99

List Words

heroes
fright
group
least
children
eight
speak
puppies
choose

Scrambled Letters Puzzle

Unscramble the letters to spell List Words. Print one letter in each box. Read down the shaded boxes to answer the riddle.

1. RIFTGH
2. ELSTA
3. LDIRHNCE
4. IPEPSPU
5. GEHIT
6. PUROG
7. KAPES
8. HOCOES
9. REHOES

Riddle: What stays hot, even in the freezer?

Answer: ___ ___ ___   ___ ___ ___ ___ ___ ___

Go for the Goal

Take your final Replay Test. Then fill in your Scoreboard. Send any misspelled words to your Word Locker.

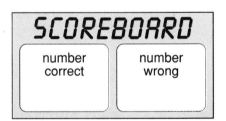

SCOREBOARD

| number correct | number wrong |

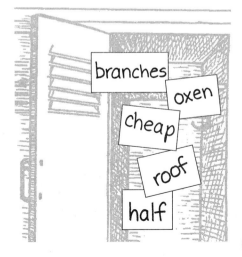

branches
oxen
cheap
roof
half

Clean Out Your Word Locker

Look in your Word Locker. Cross out each word you spelled correctly on your Final Replay Test. Circle the words you're still having trouble with. Add the words you circled to your Spelling Notebook. What do you notice about the words? Watch for those words as you write.

Name _____

/ô/

Warm Up

What hobby was known as "the hobby of kings"?

Royal Hobby

Many people like to save coins. Some people call coin collecting "the hobby of kings," **because**, at one time, only a king could afford to keep money. Most people had to spend all their money to live. Today, many people find coin collecting an easy and interesting hobby. Over five million North Americans collect coins.

To begin, all you need are a few coins and a folder in which to keep them. **Almost** any hobby shop can sell you this special kind of folder. You can keep each coin in its own special place. You might start by saving pennies. Try to get one for each year of your life.

As you learn more about coins, you will know which ones are the best to save. Look for a coin without a scratch, or **flaw.** A coin without flaws is worth more than others. However, it is not **all right** to clean a dirty coin. Rubbing wears down its face and makes it less valuable. Of course, everyone wants to find very old coins. These are hard to find and could **cost** a lot of money if you **bought** one. You could get lucky, though. You could find a valuable coin right in your own pocket.

 Say each word in dark print in the selection. Can you hear the /ô/ sound in each word?

On Your Mark

Take your Warm Up Test. Then check your spelling with the List Words on the next page.

101

The /ô/ sound can be spelled many ways:
au as in <u>because</u>   **aw** as in <u>flaw</u>
o as in <u>cost</u>   **ou** as in <u>bought</u>
a followed by **l** as in <u>already</u>

Look at the spelling of /ô/ in each List Word.

Game Plan

Spelling Lineup
Write each List Word under the correct spelling of its /ô/ sound.

LIST WORDS

1. already
2. because
3. almost
4. flaw
5. cost
6. wallet
7. laws
8. lost
9. long
10. belong
11. across
12. all right
13. bought
14. August
15. chalk
16. haul
17. awful
18. crawl
19. lawn
20. caught

au

1. _____   3. _____

2. _____   4. _____

aw

5. _____   8. _____

6. _____   9. _____

7. _____

a followed by **l**

10. _____   13. _____

11. _____   14. _____

12. _____

o or **ou**

15. _____   18. _____

16. _____   19. _____

17. _____   20. _____

Word Shape Puzzle

Write a List Word in each word shape. Use the number code to answer the riddle.

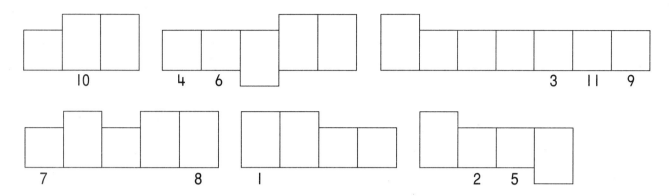

Riddle: What has four heads and four tails?

Answer: ___ ___ ___ ___   ___ ___ ___ ___ ___ ___ ___
       1   2   3   4   5   6   7   8   9 10 11

Definitions

Write the List Word that matches the meaning given.

1. rules people must obey

_____

2. missing

_____

3. to move like a worm

_____

4. not quite

_____

5. the eighth month of the year

_____

6. to be a part of something

_____

7. grass

_____

8. terrible

_____

9. to carry by wagon or truck

_____

10. by or before this time

_____

Flex Your Spelling Muscles

Writing

People enjoy collecting many different things. Do you collect something? Write a paragraph describing your collection or something you would like to collect. Use as many List Words as you can.

Proofreading

This article has eight mistakes. Use the proofreading marks to fix each mistake. Write the misspelled List Words on the lines.

Proofreading Marks

⬯ spelling mistake

^ add something

↩ take out something

Collecting baseball cards is a popular hobby akross the country. Many kids are trading cards they bowght at hobby shops. Would you like to be a collector If so, remember that some some cards cawst a lot. So, be careful not to get cawt spending too much.? You'll need to keep some change in your waulet—just in case you spot the card that will complete your collection.

1. _____

2. _____

3. _____

4. _____

5. _____

Now proofread your paragraph.
Fix any mistakes.

Go for the Goal

Take your Final Test. Then fill in your Scoreboard. Send your mistakes to the Word Locker.

SCOREBOARD

number correct	number wrong

★ ★ ★ ★ ★ ★ ★ ★ ★ **All-Star Words** ★ ★ ★ ★ ★ ★ ★ ★ ★

moth   sausage   awkward   altogether   brought

Write a song title for each All-Star Word. Then get together with a partner and compare titles.

/oi/ or /ou/

Warm Up

Where is Clown College?

Clowning Around

Have you ever wanted to be a **clown?**
Before you **join** the circus, you have to go to
a very special school for clowns in Venice,
Florida. Clown College takes only sixty
students each year. They learn to juggle and to
walk on tall poles called stilts. They also learn
how to tumble head over heels and to ride a
unicycle. That's a bike with only one wheel. Of course, they learn to fall
down and make the **crowd** laugh.

The special students who go to Clown College really **enjoy** it.
Learning to be a clown is hard work. For ten weeks, each student must
prepare a special clown character. One clown may be fat with a big **round**
face. Another may be tall with a head that comes to a **point.** The students
must plan and make their own clothes and tricks. Most important is their
makeup. Each clown has to have a different face. One will have a big, fat
nose. Another will make a giant mouth or big ears. The students wear
their "faces" all day at school to get used to being a clown.

Clown college is part of the Ringling Brothers and Barnum and
Bailey Circus. They call it "The Greatest Show on Earth." They're
not just clowning around!

Say each word in dark print in the selection. How
are the words with the /oi/ sound spelled? How
are the words with the /ou/ sound spelled?

On Your Mark

Take your Warm Up Test. Then check your spelling with
the List Words on the next page.

Pep Talk

The /oi/ sound may be spelled **oy** as in <u>toys</u> or oi as in <u>coin</u>. The /ou/ sound may be spelled **ow** as in <u>town</u> or **ou** as in <u>proud</u>. Each List Word has the /oi/ or /ou/ sound. Look at how the sound is spelled in each List Word.

LIST WORDS

1. clown
2. join
3. town
4. crowd
5. enjoy
6. round
7. loud
8. point
9. coin
10. toys
11. about
12. proud
13. allow
14. foil
15. power
16. pound
17. blouse
18. crown
19. choice
20. loyal

Game Plan

Spelling Lineup

Write each List Word under the correct heading.

oi as in <u>oil</u>

1. _____
2. _____
3. _____
4. _____
5. _____

ow as in <u>how</u>

6. _____
7. _____
8. _____
9. _____
10. _____
11. _____

oy as in <u>boy</u>

12. _____
13. _____
14. _____

ou as in <u>sound</u>

15. _____
16. _____
17. _____
18. _____
19. _____
20. _____

Word Building

Build List Words by adding or subtracting letters. Write
the List Words.

1. enter – ter + joy = _____

2. alone – one + low = _____

3. black – ack + ouse = _____

4. crown – n + d = _____

5. pouch – ch + nd = _____

6. above – ve + ut = _____

7. boys – b + t = _____

8. voice – v + ch = _____

9. sound – s + r = _____

10. joint – j + p = _____

11. royal – r + l = _____

12. brown – br + cl = _____

13. coil – l + n = _____

14. jolly – lly + in = _____

Rhyming

Write a List Word that rhymes with the underlined
clue word to complete each silly definition.

1. A place where funny people live is a <u>clown</u> _____ .

2. A group of noisy people is a _____ <u>crowd</u>.

3. A monster who cooks and eats metal things might <u>boil</u> _____ .

4. A cloud that is pleased with itself is a _____ <u>cloud</u>.

5. A sad or angry king might wear a <u>frown</u> _____ .

6. A king who is true to his country is a _____ <u>royal</u>.

7. A king who rules from the top of a castle has <u>tower</u> _____ .

Flex Your Spelling Muscles

Writing

If you could be a clown, what kind of clown would you be? How would you look? What would you do to make people laugh? Draw a picture of you as a clown. Then use the List Words to write a few sentences describing your act.

Proofreading

This poem has eleven mistakes. Use the proofreading marks to fix each mistake. Write the misspelled List Words on the lines.

the circus is coming to toun.
I can't wait to to see a clooun.
i've heard there will be lots of toiys
For all all the happy girls and boys.
I can't wait to joyn the the croud
And laugh and cheer and clap out lowd.

Now proofread your sentences. Fix any mistakes.

Proofreading Marks
⬭ spelling mistake
= capital letter
⌒ take out something

1. _____

2. _____

3. _____

4. _____

5. _____

6. _____

Go for the Goal

Take your Final Test. Then fill in your Scoreboard. Send your mistakes to the Word Locker.

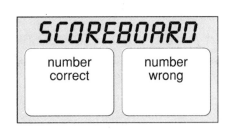

SCOREBOARD

number correct	number wrong

★ ★ ★ ★ ★ ★ ★ ★ ★ **All-Star Words** ★ ★ ★ ★ ★ ★ ★ ★ ★

avoid   doubt   destroy   spoil   drown

Work with a partner to write a story using the All-Star Words. Swap stories with other students. How did they use the All-Star Words?

Name _____

/sh/, /th/, or /th/

Warm Up

What U.S. championship did Stanley Newman win?

The Crossword Kid

In a very **short** time, Stanley Newman won $1500 and a pencil six feet long. He won these prizes thanks to a lot of practice and a **sharp** mind. Stanley finished a crossword puzzle in **thirteen** minutes and twenty seconds. He won the first U.S. Open Crossword Puzzle Championship.

The 261 final players met at New York University in New York City. They were the best "puzzlers" in the country. Their hopes were high. They didn't want **fourth** or **fifth** place. Not even second or third place would do. Each one came to win first prize. When it came to the last and hardest puzzle, only a few players were left.

In the end, Stanley Newman was the big winner. He had to **rush** to **finish** in the fifteen-minute time limit. He completed the puzzle in time! He was able to **dash** off the answers faster and better **than** anyone. He did make one small mistake. That only proved that even the best player isn't always perfect.

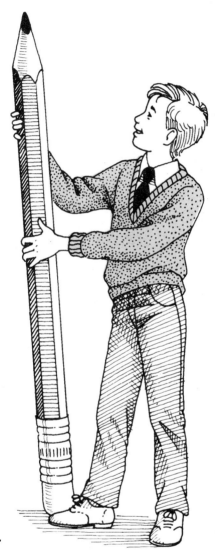

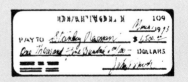 Look back at the words in dark print. Say each word. Can you find two consonants together in each word that make only one sound?

On Your Mark

Take your Warm Up Test. Then check your spelling with the List Words on the next page.

Pep Talk

The consonant pairs **sh** and **th** are called **consonant digraphs.** They spell the special sounds you hear in <u>short</u>, <u>rush</u>, <u>thumb</u>, and <u>that</u>. Listen for the sounds the letters **sh** and **th** spell in the List Words.

LIST WORDS

1. short
2. thaw
3. sharp
4. thirty
5. fourth
6. fifth
7. rush
8. dash
9. than
10. that
11. thinking
12. push
13. shape
14. thirteen
15. finish
16. thumb
17. sixth
18. shadow
19. shine
20. shovel

Game Plan

Spelling Lineup

Write the List Words that begin with **sh.**

1. _____   4. _____

2. _____   5. _____

3. _____   6. _____

Write the List Words that end with **sh.**

7. _____   9. _____

8. _____   10. _____

Write the List Words that begin with **th.**

11. _____   15. _____

12. _____   16. _____

13. _____   17. _____

14. _____

Write the List Words that end with **th.**

18. _____   20. _____

19. _____

Dictionary

Write the List Words that would appear on a dictionary page that has the guide words shown.

In a dictionary, **guide words** at the top of each page tell you the first and last words that appear on that page. **dash / daze**

run/show

1. _____

2. _____

3. _____

4. _____   6. _____

5. _____   7. _____

side/Thursday

8. _____   12. _____

9. _____   13. _____

10. _____   14. _____

11. _____   15. _____

Synonyms

Write the List Word that means the same as the word or numeral given.

1. scoop _____   10. a dark shape _____

2. 5th _____   11. mark (–) _____

3. glow _____   12. shove _____

4. 4th _____

5. end _____

6. melt _____

7. pointed _____

8. 30 _____

9. 13 _____

Flex Your Spelling Muscles

Writing

Puzzles are a lot of fun, and there are many kinds to choose from. There are crossword puzzles, word search puzzles, and jigsaw puzzles just to name a few. Use the List Words to describe your favorite puzzle. Tell why you like it.

Proofreading

The following article has eight mistakes. Use the proofreading marks to fix each mistake. Write the misspelled List Words on the lines.

<table>
<tr><td colspan="2">Proofreading Marks</td></tr>
<tr><td>⬭</td><td>spelling mistake</td></tr>
<tr><td>≡</td><td>capital letter</td></tr>
<tr><td>∧</td><td>add something</td></tr>
</table>

arthur Wynne created the first crossword puzzle in 1913. His idea came from agame his grandfather had taught him called Magic Square. In a very shorte time, wynne's own puzzle began to take shaip. When it was completed, he knew thet it would take a sharpe mind to solve it. Wynne's puzzle was so popular that soon people everywhere were in a rushe to buy crossword puzzle books.

1. _____

2. _____

3. _____

4. _____

5. _____

Now proofread what you wrote about your favorite puzzle. Fix any mistakes.

Go for the Goal

Take your Final Test. Then fill in your Scoreboard. Send your mistakes to the Word Locker.

SCOREBOARD

number correct	number wrong

★ ★ ★ ★ ★ ★ ★ ★ ★ **All-Star Words** ★ ★ ★ ★ ★ ★ ★ ★ ★

breathe   shoulder   shiver   thief   selfish

Try to use all five All-Star Words in a single sentence. Then get together with a partner and compare sentences.

Name _____

/ch/, /hw/, or /h/

Warm Up

What is *nanomin?*

Gift from the Creator

Each September, the Ojibwa Indians of Minnesota hold a very special harvest of a very special grain. They call it *nanomin,* **which** means "the gift from the creator." Nanomin is a grain not only **rich** in vitamins and nutrients, but it's also delicious. It's used in soups, salads, breads, cakes, and even as breakfast cereal. Also called wild rice, this wild grain from Minnesota is said to be the world's finest.

At daybreak, hundreds of canoes glide across the marshes among the tall green stalks. In each canoe there are two people. One partner pushes a pole against the pond's bottom to move the boat slowly through the marsh. The other partner uses a pair of slender sticks to bend the stalks of grain over the side of the canoe. The sticks are then used to **whack** the stalks, dislodging the rice into the canoe.

The harvesting of the wild rice is a cause for celebration of their Ojibwa's traditions. As one harvester said, "the sweet thing about the wild rice harvest is that it brings families together."

Look back at the words in dark print. What sound does the consonant digraph **ch** make? What sounds does the consonant digraph **wh** make?

On Your Mark

Take your Warm Up Test. Then check your spelling with the List Words on the next page.

Consonant digraphs are pairs of consonants, such as **ch** or **wh,** that make one sound when they are written together in a syllable. You can hear the /ch/ sound in <u>each</u> and the /hw/ sound in <u>whale</u>. In <u>who</u> and <u>whole</u>, the **w** is silent, but you hear the **h.**

LIST WORDS

1. wheel
2. whale
3. everywhere
4. which
5. each
6. check
7. while
8. chewy
9. rich
10. chapter
11. chart
12. catch
13. whisper
14. who
15. whole
16. bench
17. whisk
18. whack
19. whether
20. pinch

Game Plan

Spelling Lineup

Write each List Word under the correct sound of its consonant digraph. One word will be used twice.

/ /

1. _____   6. _____

2. _____   7. _____

3. _____   8. _____

4. _____   9. _____

5. _____   10. _____

/hw/

11. _____   15. _____

12. _____   16. _____

13. _____   18. _____

14. _____   19. _____

/h/

20. _____   21. _____

Dictionary

Write the List Word for each sound-spelling given.

> In a dictionary, a **sound-spelling** is given for each entry word. It tells you how to pronounce a word. **each** (ēch)

1. (choo´ ē) _____

2. (bench) _____

3. (hwisk) _____

4. (chap´ tər) _____

5. (kach) _____   7. (hwīl) _____

6. (chärt) _____   8. (ev´ rē hwer´) _____

Scrambled Letters

Unscramble the letters to make List Words.
Then use the number code to answer the riddle.

1. chawk __ __ __ __ __
            10

2. ohw __ __ __
         4

3. thewreh __ __ __ __ __ __ __
                        2

4. priwseh __ __ __ __ __ __ __
                           6

5. chinp __ __ __ __ __
                  5

6. hawel __ __ __ __ __
              8 11

7. loweh __ __ __ __ __
               9 3

8. elehw __ __ __ __ __
          1   7

Find the letter with the number 1 under it.
Print that letter on the line below that has
the number 1 under it. Do the same for
numbers 2 through 11.

Riddle: What do you say when you meet a three-headed monster?

Answer: __ __ __ __ __   __ __ __ __ __   __ __ __ __ __
            1 2 3 3 4   5 6 7 8 9   10 11 7 8 9

Flex Your Spelling Muscles

Writing

Many foods are made of rice. There are rice cakes, rice pudding, and rice cereal. Use the List Words to write a paragraph describing the rice foods you like.

Proofreading

This paragraph has nine mistakes. Use the proofreading marks to fix each mistake. Write the misspelled List Words on the lines.

Proofreading Marks
⬯ spelling mistake
⊙ add period
⌇ take out something

In a Hopi family's cornfield, wich they have farmed for many years, plants are evreeware. The Hopi dig small holes in the ground and put kernels in in eech hole They chek the plants daily to keep pests away If there is enough rain, the harvest will be be ritch.

1. _____   4. _____

2. _____   5. _____

3. _____

Now proofread your paragraph. Fix any mistakes.

Go for the Goal

Take your Final Test. Then fill in your Scoreboard. Send your mistakes to the Word Locker.

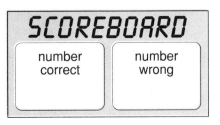

SCOREBOARD

number correct	number wrong

★ ★ ★ ★ ★ ★ ★ ★ **All-Star Words** ★ ★ ★ ★ ★ ★ ★ ★ ★

whirl   whine   champion   witch   somewhat

Write a sentence for each word. Then scramble the letters in the All-Star Words. Trade papers with a partner. Unscramble the All-Star Word in each sentence and write it correctly.

Consonant Clusters

LESSON
29

Warm Up

Where was the first swamp buggy race held?

Mud Machines

Splash! It's another buggy in the mud. What do you think is going on? You could call it a mud rodeo. Some people say it's the dirtiest race on earth. It happens twice a year during Swamp Buggy Days in Naples, Florida. In late winter, just before **spring,** and again in the fall, the swamp buggies tune up for action.

Swamp buggies were once used for hunting in the swamps of Florida. Then over thirty years ago, a man named Ed Frank started the swamp buggy races. The first one was held in a muddy sweet potato **patch.** Through the years, the buggies got better and faster. They are all crazy-looking machines with big tires and **strong** engines.

Today the buggies race through "Mile-O-Mud" track. It runs through the swamps like a big figure eight. The drivers have to make sharp turns and look out for big holes. There are lots of spills and **thrills.** Mud sprays in all directions and the fans **scream.** It's quite a sight to see, and it's all good, but not clean, fun!

Look back at the words in dark print. Say each word. Can you find the three consonants together in each word?

On Your Mark

Take your Warm Up Test. Then check your spelling with the List Words on the next page.

Pep Talk

Three consonants together in a word make a **consonant cluster.** In many List Words, **s** forms a cluster with two other letters. In some List Words, /ch/ or /th/ forms a cluster with another letter.

1. splash
2. spring
3. patch
4. strong
5. thrills
6. spray
7. scream
8. throw
9. string
10. struck
11. screen
12. itch
13. pitch
14. spread
15. strawberry
16. stream
17. split
18. scratch
19. ditch
20. thread

Game Plan

Spelling Lineup

Finish each List Word by writing a consonant cluster.

1. _____ ash
2. _____ ead
3. _____ ing
4. _____ ong
5. _____ it
6. _____ awberry
7. _____ ead
8. _____ ills
9. _____ ing
10. _____ ow
11. _____ pi
12. _____ pa
13. _____ atch
14. _____ uck
15. _____ di
16. _____ i
17. _____ eam
18. _____ ay
19. _____ een
20. _____ eam

Alphabetical Order

Write the List Words in alphabetical order.

| spring | splash | spread | strong | scratch | spray |

1. _____   3. _____   5. _____

2. _____   4. _____   6. _____

Puzzle

Write a List Word to solve each clue. Then read
down the shaded boxes to answer the riddle.

1. This word names a fruit.   __ __ __ __ __ __ __ __

2. This will keep flies out of your home.   __ __ __ __ __ __

3. This is a loud yell.   __ __ __ __ __ __

4. This means "hit."   __ __ __ __ __ __

5. This word names a deep hole.   __ __ __ __ __

Riddle: What did the strawberry patch say to the rain?

Answer: If you keep this up, my

name will __ __   __ __ __ !

Classification

Write the List Word that belongs in each group.

1. fix, mend, _____   5. throw, toss, _____

2. skin, rash, _____   6. joy, excitement, _____

3. fall, winter, _____   7. string, ribbon, _____

4. share, divide, _____   8. brook, river, _____

Flex Your Spelling Muscles

Writing

Imagine that you just attended the races at Swamp Buggy Days. Write a brief news report about what you saw. Include lots of colorful details. Use as many List Words as you can.

Proofreading

The poster below has ten mistakes. Use the proofreading marks to fix each mistake. Write the misspelled List Words on the lines.

Proofreading Marks
⬭ spelling mistake
∧ add something
/ make small letter

Where can you go to find thrilz and chills
Where else but Strawbarry Pache Beach for the annual Spreeng Fling.
Watch the amazing dune buggy racers splasch through each wet, sandy dicth.
Skream for the winners when they reach the Finish line.
It all happens on June 23, beginning at 10 A.m.

1. _____

2. _____

3. _____

4. _____

5. _____

6. _____

7. _____

Now proofread your news report. Fix any mistakes.

Go for the Goal

Take your Final Test. Then fill in your Scoreboard. Send your mistakes to the Word Locker.

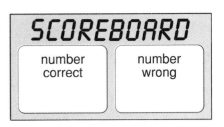

SCOREBOARD

number correct	number wrong

★ ★ ★ ★ ★ ★ ★ ★ **All-Star Words** ★ ★ ★ ★ ★ ★ ★ ★

sprang   scramble   stranger   throne   hatch

With your partner, write a definition for each All-Star Word. Then look them up in the glossary. Do your meanings match? Now use each All-Star Word in a sentence.

Name _____

Instant Replay • Lessons 25–29

LESSON
30

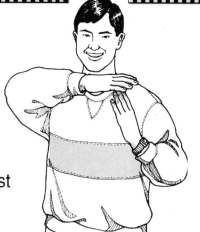

Time Out

Take another look at the /ô/, /oi/, and /ou/ sounds, consonant digraphs, and consonant clusters.

Check Your Word Locker

Look at the words in your Word Locker. Write your most troublesome words for Lessons 25–29.

_____

_____

Practice writing your troublesome words with a partner. Try writing the letters for each word in a tray of sand, salt, or sugar. Your partner can check your spelling as you write.

Lesson 25

The /ô/ sound can be spelled many ways as in <u>flaw</u>, <u>because</u>, <u>already</u>, and <u>bought</u>.

List Words

almost
laws
August
wallet
all right
crawl

Write a List Word that matches each clue.

1. summer month

_____

2. rules

_____

3. not quite

_____

4. to creep

_____

5. money holder

_____

6. good enough

_____

121

Listen for the /ͻi/ sound in <u>join</u> and <u>toys</u>, and for the /ͻu/ sound in <u>loud</u> and <u>town</u>.

List Words

crowd
point
about
power
choice
loyal

Write each List Word under the correct heading.

one syllable

1. _____

2. _____

3. _____

two syllables

4. _____

5. _____

6. _____

Two consonants can join together in a word to form a **consonant digraph,** as in <u>thaw</u>, <u>then</u>, and <u>short</u>.

List Words

fourth
push
thumb
thinking
that
shine

Write a List Word that rhymes with each word given.

1. mine _____   4. north _____

2. hum _____   5. bush _____

3. flat _____   6. sinking _____

Listen for the consonant digraphs in <u>chewy</u>, <u>whale</u>, and <u>who</u>.

List Words

which
check
chart
catch
whisper
whole

Write the List Words in alphabetical order.

1. _____   4. _____

2. _____   5. _____

3. _____   6. _____

Three consonants can join together to form a cluster. Listen for the **consonant clusters** in <u>split</u>, <u>itch</u>, and <u>thrills</u>.

List Words

spring
scream
stream
strong
throw
thread

Read the first two underlined words in each sentence. Write the List Word that goes with the third underlined word in the same way.

1. <u>Big</u> is to <u>large</u> as <u>yell</u> is to _____ .

2. <u>Cut</u> is to <u>scissors</u> as <u>sew</u> is to _____ .

3. <u>Up</u> is to <u>down</u> as <u>catch</u> is to _____ .

4. <u>On</u> is to <u>off</u> as <u>weak</u> is to _____ .

5. <u>Winter</u> is to <u>summer</u> as <u>fall</u> is to _____ .

6. <u>Road</u> is to <u>street</u> as <u>creek</u> is to _____ .

List Words

almost
shine
fourth
whisper
loyal
crowd
point
thumb
which
thread

Write a List Word to finish each sentence.

1. My mother says it's not polite to _____ at people.

2. Our baseball team took _____ place in the league.

3. You should always _____ quietly in a library.

4. The _____ was excited when the circus finally started.

5. _____ everyone likes to eat hamburgers.

6. I broke my _____ playing ball.

7. _____ way does this bus go?

8. _____ fans never miss a game.

9. May I borrow a needle and _____?

10. I waxed my bicycle to make it _____.

Go for the Goal

Take your Final Replay Test. Then fill in your Scoreboard. Send any misspelled words to your Word Locker.

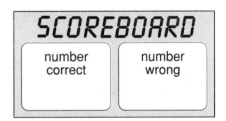

SCOREBOARD

number correct	number wrong

haul
enjoy
fifth
whack
patch

Clean Out Your Locker

Look in your Word Locker. Cross out each word you spelled correctly on your Final Replay Test. Circle the words you're still having trouble with. Add the words you circled to your Spelling Notebook. What do you notice about the words? Watch for those words as you write.

Consonant Digraphs

Warm Up

What are hieroglyphs?

The Art of Writing

Over 5,000 years ago, the Egyptians started to write their spoken language down. As with the beginnings of many written languages, the Egyptians **wrote** their language using pictures. These pictures are called hieroglyphs. Each hieroglyph stands for a different sound. Several hieroglyphs can stand for a letter, especially when it comes to vowels. That's because vowels have more than one sound.

Unlike English, hieroglyphs can be written in more than one direction. They can be written from left to right, like English, or right to left, like Arabic and Hebrew. They can also be written from top to bottom, like Chinese. You might ask how the ancient Egyptians kept **track** of which direction in which to read. They **knew** by the pictures themselves. If the sign for a letter faced left, they started reading from the left. If the **sign** faced right, they started reading from the right.

A **writer** using Egyptian hieroglyphs would probably have a **rough** time telling a story. You would not only have to know how to write, but also how to draw!

Hieroglyphs that spell the word <u>read</u>.

r

ea

d

Look back at the words in dark print. Say each word. Can you find two consonants together in each word that make only one sound?

On Your Mark

Take your Warm Up Test. Then check your spelling with the List Words on the next page.

125

LIST WORDS

1. school
2. wrote
3. phone
4. knew
5. sign
6. knots
7. wrong
8. knee
9. knife
10. wreck
11. wrap
12. knock
13. rough
14. laugh
15. elephant
16. cough
17. wren
18. writer
19. graph
20. track

Game Plan

Spelling Lineup

Say each sound. Write the List Words that spell that sound with a digraph. Then circle the digraph in each word. Some words will be written more than once.

/n/

1. _____
2. _____
3. _____
4. _____
5. _____
6. _____

/r/

7. _____
8. _____
9. _____
10. _____
11. _____
12. _____

/f/

13. _____
14. _____
15. _____
16. _____
17. _____
18. _____

/k/

19. _____
20. _____
21. _____
22. _____

Puzzle

Fill in the crossword puzzle by writing
a List Word to answer each clue.

ACROSS
2. the bend in your leg
3. not correct
4. a person who
   writes
5. felt sure about
8. a place to learn
9. a chart

DOWN
1. used a pen
   and paper
2. rap on a door
3. a small bird
4. something that
   is a mess
6. to put a cover around
7. take medicine for this

Missing Words

Write a List Word from the box to finish each phrase.

| knots | knife | elephant | rough | laugh |

1. as sharp as a _____

2. as ___ as sandpaper _____

3. as big as an _____

4. the last _____

5. all tied up in _____

Flex Your Spelling Muscles

Writing

Have you ever wanted to create your own secret language? If so, here's your chance. First, use the List Words to write a secret message. Then draw pictures or symbols to illustrate your message.

Proofreading

This diary entry has eleven mistakes. Use the proofreading marks to fix each mistake. Write the misspelled List Words on the lines.

Proofreading Marks
- spelling mistake
- add period
- take out something

Dear Diary,

Last week, my teacher called me on the fone and asked me to to write an article for the sckool paper. I was so excited! First, I made an outline to keep trak of my ideas Next, I wroat a ruff draft. Then, I proofread it it and fixed my mistakes. Finally, it was time to sine my name and turn it in. My teacher loved it! Well, Diary, today it appeared in the paper. Now I know what I want to be when I grow up—a riter

1. ____________
2. ____________
3. ____________
4. ____________
5. ____________
6. ____________
7. ____________

Now proofread your secret message. Fix any mistakes.

Go for the Goal

Take your Final Test. Then fill in your Scoreboard. Send your mistakes to the Word Locker.

SCOREBOARD	
number correct	number wrong

★ ★ ★ ★ ★ ★ ★ ★ ★ **All-Star Words** ★ ★ ★ ★ ★ ★ ★ ★ ★

knit wrinkle tough cricket anchor

Write a story using all the words. Then scramble the letters in the All-Star Words. Trade papers with a partner. Unscramble the All-Star Words in the story.

Name _____

Prefixes un, dis

Warm Up

What is the real name for a shooting star?

Shooting Stars?

Did you know that shooting stars aren't really stars at all? They start out as cold chunks of rock speeding through space. Often one will get caught in the air around the earth and start falling. As it races through the earth's air, it gets so hot it glows. Scientists call this shooting star a meteor.

Most of these glowing space rocks burn up in the air and **disappear.** The very few that ever reach the earth are called meteorites. These special rocks often go **unseen** on the ground. Wind and weather break them into smaller pieces. You would probably be **unable** to tell a meteorite from an ordinary earth rock.

Scientists have been able to **discover** many meteorites in Antarctica, near the South Pole. The dark rocks are easy to see on the empty ice fields. The cold, dry air has kept many meteorites **unchanged** for thousands of years. Unlike those in other places, the meteorites in Antarctica have been **untouched** by **unclean** air and by weather.

That shooting star you see may not make your wish come true. Don't be too **unhappy.** Scientists say it could unlock some secrets of the planets and outer space.

Look back at the words in dark print. These words have word parts, or prefixes, added to the front of them to make new words. Name the two prefixes.

On Your Mark

Take your Warm Up Test. Then check your spelling with the List Words on the next page.

129

Pep Talk

A **prefix** is a word part added to the beginning of a **root word.** It changes the root's meaning. The prefixes **dis** and **un** mean <u>not</u> or <u>the</u> <u>opposite</u>, as in <u>unseen</u> and <u>dislike</u>. Think about the meaning of each List Word.

LIST WORDS

1. unseen
2. unable
3. discover
4. unload
5. unclean
6. unsure
7. uneven
8. dislike
9. displease
10. distrust
11. unwrap
12. untrue
13. unlucky
14. unchanged
15. untouched
16. disobey
17. disorder
18. unbutton
19. unpaid
20. disappear

Game Plan

Spelling Lineup

Write each List Word under the correct heading.

words with the prefix **dis**

1. _____   5. _____

2. _____   6. _____

3. _____   7. _____

4. _____

words with the prefix **un**

8. _____   15. _____

9. _____   16. _____

10. _____   17. _____

11. _____   18. _____

12. _____   19. _____

13. _____   20. _____

14. _____

Synonyms

Write the List Word that means the same as the word given.

1. find _____

2. false _____

3. mess _____

4. vanish _____

5. hate _____

6. dirty _____

7. annoy _____

8. uncertain _____

Scrambled Letters

Unscramble the letters to spell each root word.
Write the List Word that contains it.

1. doutech _____

2. aldo _____

3. praw _____

4. hangced _____

5. boye _____

6. neev _____

7. surtt _____

8. tunobt _____

9. nese _____

10. apid _____

11. culky _____

12. bale _____

13. nalec _____

14. rocev _____

15. retu _____

16. dorer _____

17. leapse _____

18. rapepa _____

19. ruse _____

20. eikl _____

Flex Your Spelling Muscles

Writing

Have you ever wished on a star? What did you wish for? Write a few sentences telling about your wish. Use as many List Words as you can.

Proofreading

This diary entry below has nine mistakes. Use the proofreading marks to fix the mistakes. Then write the misspelled List Words on the lines.

Proofreading Marks
- ⬯ spelling mistake
- ≡ capital letter
- ⩔ add apostrophe

last night I was unabel to sleep so I sat up and watched the stars. Suddenly I saw something streak through the sky and then disappeer. I was surprised and a little unshure of what Id seen. So, I listened to the news this morning hoping to diskover the answer. sure enough, the news reported the sighting of a meteor last night. what a relief! Now I know I wasnt seeing things.

1. _____   3. _____

2. _____   4. _____

Now proofread your sentences. Fix any mistakes.

Go for the Goal

Take your Final Test. Then fill in your Scoreboard. Send your mistakes to the Word Locker.

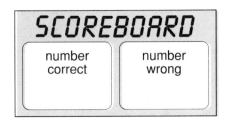

SCOREBOARD

number correct	number wrong

★ ★ ★ ★ ★ ★ ★ ★ ★ **All-Star Words** ★ ★ ★ ★ ★ ★ ★ ★ ★

unusual   uneasy   unprepared   disrespect   distaste

Write a sentence for each All-Star Word. Trade sentences with a partner. Circle the prefixes in the All-Star Words and tell their meanings.

Name _____

Prefix re

Warm Up

Why did it take so long for Bartholdi to finish the statue?

Bigger Than Life

She stands in New York Harbor. She is more than twenty times larger than life. One of her fingers is taller than a person, and one fingernail is 13 inches wide! She's the Statue of Liberty! Her full name is "Liberty Enlightening the World." People often **rename** her "Miss Liberty."

The statue was a gift to the United States from France. In the 1700's both countries had fought to free themselves from the rule of kings. The French people wanted to **remind** Americans of the friendship and freedom they now shared.

The artist, Frederic Auguste Bartholdi, took nearly ten years to finish the statue. He had to make and remake his plan on paper. Then he had to build and **rebuild** models until the statue pleased him. First, he made a small clay model in Paris. Then he built one 36 feet tall and marked it off into 300 pieces. Each piece was then made in a larger size and sent to America. In 1886, on an island in New York Harbor, the giant puzzle was put together.

Even today the Statue of Liberty stands proudly to **retell** the world that America is free. No other statue could ever **replace** it.

Take a look at the words in dark print in the selection. How does the prefix **re** change the meaning of each root word?

On Your Mark

Take your Warm Up Test. Then check your spelling with the List Words on the next page.

133

Pep Talk

The prefix **re** can mean <u>again</u> or <u>back</u>.
re + <u>tell</u> = <u>retell</u>, meaning "tell again"
re + <u>pay</u> = <u>repay</u>, meaning "pay back"

Think about the meaning of **re** in each of the List Words.

1. rename
2. remind
3. refresh
4. retell
5. rewrite
6. replay
7. repay
8. refill
9. reload
10. rerun
11. replace
12. redo
13. replant
14. renew
15. rebuild
16. recopy
17. regroup
18. rethink
19. rework
20. reform

Game Plan

Spelling Lineup

Add the prefix **re** to each of these roots to form a List Word. Write the List Words.

1. form _____
2. build _____
3. load _____
4. mind _____
5. place _____
6. think _____
7. group _____
8. plant _____
9. write _____
10. fresh _____
11. copy _____
12. do _____
13. tell _____

14. new _____
15. pay _____
16. fill _____
17. run _____
18. work _____
19. play _____
20. name _____

Scrambled Letters Puzzle

Fill in the crossword puzzle by unscrambling each set of letters to write a List Word.

ACROSS
3. RETWIRE
6. RECLEAP
7. DORE
8. YAPER

DOWN
1. GROPURE
2. EMANER
3. PRAYLE
4. PORCEY
5. KREROW

Rhyming

The root of a List Word rhymes with each of these words. Write the complete List Word.

1. can't _____

2. floppy _____

3. sun _____

4. ink _____

5. face _____

6. sell _____

7. toad _____

8. warm _____

9. flight _____

10. loop _____

11. hill _____

12. kind _____

13. mesh _____

14. filled _____

Flex Your Spelling Muscles

Writing

There are many monuments and statues that honor people or events in our history. Write a paragraph about one you have visited or know about. Use as many List Words as you can.

This article has nine mistakes. Use the proofreading marks to fix the mistakes. Then write the misspelled List Words on the lines.

Proofreading Marks
◯ spelling mistake
∧ add something
/ make small letter

   Can a mountain be made into a Monument Of course it can Mount Rushmore, on which the faces of four American presidents are carved, should reemind you of that fact. Nearby, another mountain will someday reetel the story of Crazy Horse a Sioux warrior. The image of this famous warrior and his horse will eventually replase an ordinary mountain. Unfortunately, the Artist died before he could complete his sculpture. The artist's wife and family plan to reneu and complete this incredible work of art.

1. _____

2. _____

3. _____

4. _____

Now proofread your paragraph. Fix any mistakes.

Go for the Goal

Take your Final Test. Then fill in your Scoreboard. Send your mistakes to the Word Locker.

SCOREBOARD

number correct	number wrong

★ ★ ★ ★ ★ ★ ★ ★ **All-Star Words** ★ ★ ★ ★ ★ ★ ★ ★

reappear   rewire   reapply   reassign   reorder

Use the All-Star Words to create a crossword puzzle. Make a grid and then write a clue for each word. Swap papers with a partner. Can you fill in the puzzle with the correct All-Star Words?

Contractions

Warm Up

Who or what is Ursus horribilis?

Ursus Horribilis

One night not too long ago, a group of campers at Yellowstone National Park had an unwelcome visitor to their barbecue—a yearling grizzly bear. A yearling is a grizzly **that's** about 1 year old. This 170 pound youngster walked into the picnic area, and calmly roamed from table to table, enjoying the feast. Of course, the terrified picnickers **didn't** stay around to watch the grizzly help himself to 180 steaks, rice, coleslaw, baked beans, and watermelon!

Park rangers have nicknamed this grizzly Ursus horribilis Number 181. Rangers have captured him, and moved him to another area of the park. It is the park's policy to relocate bears, so that they **won't** become dependent on human food. Rangers try to keep human contact to a minimum, so that the bears will stick to natural foods like berries and rodents, and stay away from the things they **shouldn't** eat, like steaks!

Yellowstone's bear expert says that **there's** a "good possibility" Number 181 will return to the scene of his crime. He claims that bears never forget where there's a good meal, and 181's last picnic was probably the best he'll ever have.

Look back at the words in dark print. What do you notice about their spelling?

On Your Mark

Take your Warm Up Test. Then check your spelling with the List Words on the next page.

All the List Words are **contractions.** A contraction is a short way to write two words. Use an **apostrophe** (') to show where letters have been left out of a contraction. <u>I</u>'d is a contraction for <u>I would</u>. <u>He</u>'s is a contraction for <u>he is</u>.

LIST WORDS

1. there's
2. haven't
3. he's
4. couldn't
5. that's
6. I'll
7. isn't
8. didn't
9. they're
10. we'll
11. mustn't
12. shouldn't
13. wasn't
14. won't
15. I'd
16. wouldn't
17. don't
18. I've
19. you've
20. doesn't

Game Plan

Spelling Lineup
Write the List Words. Remember to include the apostrophe in each word.

1. _____
2. _____
3. _____
4. _____
5. _____
6. _____
7. _____
8. _____
9. _____
10. _____
11. _____
12. _____
13. _____
14. _____
15. _____
16. _____
17. _____
18. _____
19. _____
20. _____

there's = there is
don't = do not
I've = I have

Contractions

Circle the two words in each sentence that can
be shortened into a contraction to make a
List Word. Then write the List Words.

1. You must not tell my secret. _____

2. We have not seen Bill all day. _____

3. Pedro is not feeling well. _____

4. You have made me happy. _____

5. That is a pretty dress you're wearing. _____

6. They are all going to a party. _____

7. I have never been to the zoo. _____

Alphabetical Order

Write each group of List Words in alphabetical order.

| doesn't   didn't   don't | | we'll   won't   wasn't |

1. _____   4. _____

2. _____   5. _____

3. _____   6. _____

Rhyming

Write the three List Words that rhyme with each other.

1. _____   2. _____   3. _____

Flex Your Spelling Muscles

Writing

Imagine that you are the bear that raided the picnic area. Write a paragraph telling your side of the story. Use as many List Words as you can.

Proofreading

This poem has eight mistakes. Use the proofreading marks to fix each mistake. Circle the List Words that are incorrect, then write them correctly on the lines.

Theres a bear in in the woods I know for sure.
Hes black and covered with fuzzy fur.
Youve never seen such a great, big beast.
Id say he's ten feet tall at at the very least.
Now I think that bear is is chasing me.
So Ill have to run and climb a tree.

Now proofread your paragraph. Fix any mistakes.

Proofreading Marks

᠈   add apostrophe

᠊ᐒ   take out something

1. _____

2. _____

3. _____

4. _____

5. _____

Go for the Goal

Take your Final Test. Then fill in your Scoreboard. Send your mistakes to the Word Locker.

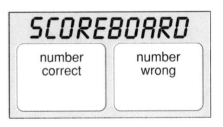

SCOREBOARD

number correct	number wrong

★ ★ ★ ★ ★ ★ ★ ★ ★ **All-Star Words** ★ ★ ★ ★ ★ ★ ★ ★ ★

hasn't   they'll   where's   how's   would've

With a partner, write a paragraph using each All-Star Word in its two-word form. Trade papers with other students. Rewrite their paragraph with the correct All-Star Word contractions.

Name _____

Homonyms

Warm Up

What is the "Hunter's Bend"?

New Knot

Girl Scouts! Boy Scouts! Now **hear** this! Let me tell you about a **great** knot. It was invented in England by Dr. Edward Hunter. Years ago, he was playing with some string and **tied** it by accident.

"I put two ends opposite each other," he said. "I made loops on each end and pulled them through one another. It was very even and easy **to** tie."

The doctor thought someone must have **made** such a knot before. After many years, he took his knot to the Maritime Museum in London. There he found books filled with pictures of **too** many knots to count. A man helped him look back over 300 years of sailors' knots. They did not see any knot exactly like Dr. Hunter's. In fact, no one anywhere knew of a knot like his.

This knot has a shape all its own. It is very useful. It can be used both on land and sea. The knot went into the books. Dr. Hunter can be proud. The knot was named the "Hunter's Bend."

 Look back at the words in dark print. Which words sound the same but have different spellings? Which words sound the same as <u>here</u>, <u>grate</u>, <u>tide</u>, and <u>maid</u>?

On Your Mark

Take your Warm Up Test. Then check your spelling with the List Words on the next page.

Pep Talk

Homonyms are words that sound alike but have different meanings and different spellings. The words <u>two</u>, <u>to</u>, and <u>too</u> are homonyms. Find the pairs or groups of homonyms in the List Words.

LIST WORDS

1. hear
2. here
3. tied
4. tide
5. your
6. you're
7. hour
8. our
9. sail
10. sale
11. two
12. to
13. too
14. pair
15. pear
16. pare
17. maid
18. made
19. great
20. grate

Game Plan

Spelling Lineup

Write the List Words that contain the vowel sounds given.

/ā/ as in <u>say</u>

1. _____
2. _____
3. _____
4. _____
5. _____
6. _____

/ir/ as in <u>year</u>

7. _____
8. _____

/o͞o/ as in <u>food</u>

9. _____
10. _____
11. _____

/er/ as in <u>care</u>

12. _____
13. _____
14. _____

/ôr/ as in <u>for</u>

15. _____
16. _____

/ī/ as in <u>side</u>

17. _____
18. _____

/ou/ as in <u>found</u>

19. _____
20. _____

142   Lesson 35 ■ Homonyms

Definitions

Write the List Word that matches the meaning given.

1. also   _____

2. cut or trim   _____

3. a sea change   _____

4. knotted   _____

5. use ears   _____

6. boat part   _____

7. a fruit   _____

8. metal frame   _____

9. in this place   _____

10. big   _____

11. sixty minutes   _____

12. a set   _____

13. low prices   _____

14. a contraction   _____

15. house cleaner   _____

16. a number   _____

17. toward   _____

18. built   _____

Homonyms

Write two List Words that are homonyms to answer each riddle.

1. What did the boy say when he saw the fireplace grill?

   What a _____ _____ !

2. What did the girl ask the cook to do?

   Please _____ the skin off this _____ .

3. What happened to the messy bed in the hotel room?

   The _____ _____ it.

4. What did the people sitting at the concert say?

   We can really _____

   well _____ .

Flex Your Spelling Muscles

Writing

Imagine that you are a sailor in a boat on the open sea. Write a story about your journey. Use as many List Words as you can.

Proofreading

This movie poster has eleven mistakes. Use the proofreading marks to fix each mistake. Circle the List Words that are used incorrectly. Then write the correct List Words on the lines.

Proofreading Marks

⸙ add apostrophe

⸂ take out something

You wont want to miss hour grate new movie called "Sea Voyage." Itll have you and you're friends on the edge of your seats. It begins when two friends go go for a sale in their new boat. Their trip, which was to only last an our, takes a sudden turn when the tied takes them them far out to sea. After being lost for too weeks they finally make it back home.

1. _____
2. _____
3. _____
4. _____
5. _____
6. _____
7. _____

Now proofread your story. Fix any mistakes.

Go for the Goal

Take your Final Test. Then fill in your Scoreboard. Send your mistakes to the Word Locker.

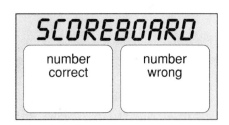

SCOREBOARD

| number correct | number wrong |

★ ★ ★ ★ ★ ★ ★ ★ **All-Star Words** ★ ★ ★ ★ ★ ★ ★ ★

cent   sent   scent   blue   blew

Write a story using each word. Then mix up the All-Star Words. Swap papers with a partner. Rewrite their story using the All-Star Words correctly.

Instant Replay • Lessons 31–35

Time Out

Take another look at consonant digraphs, prefixes, contractions, and homonyms.

Check Your Word Locker

Look at the words in your Word Locker. Write your troublesome words for Lessons 31 through 35.

_____

_____

Practice writing your troublesome words with a partner. Take turns dividing the words into syllables as your partner spells them aloud.

Lesson 31

A **consonant digraph** is two consonants together that make one sound, as in <u>knot</u>, <u>wrote</u>, <u>cough</u>, and <u>phone</u>.

List Words
knew
wreck
rough
wrong
wrap
laugh

Write a List Word that means the opposite of each word given.

1. fix _____

2. right _____

3. forgot _____

4. smooth _____

5. unwrap _____

6. cry _____

145

A **prefix** is a word part that is added to the beginning of a root word, as in <u>unable</u> and <u>discover</u>.

List Words
disobey
untrue
unbutton
unclean
displease
unlucky

Write each List Word under the number of syllables it contains.

2 syllables

1. _____

2. _____

3. _____

3 syllables

4. _____

5. _____

6. _____

The **prefix re** can mean <u>again</u> or <u>back</u>, as in <u>retell</u> and <u>repay</u>.

List Words
rename
redo
replace
reform
refill
renew

Look at each set of guide words. Decide which List Words go between each set. Then write them in alphabetical order.

rebuild/regroup

1. _____

2. _____

3. _____

remind/replant

4. _____

5. _____

6. _____

A **contraction** is a word made by writing two words together and leaving out one or more letters. An **apostrophe** shows where letters are missing, as in I'll.

List Words
there's
couldn't
doesn't
he's
they're
I'd

Write a List Word that rhymes with each word given.

1. wasn't

_____

2. bears

_____

3. hair

_____

4. wide

_____

5. bees

_____

6. wouldn't

_____

Homonyms are words that sound alike, but have different meanings and spellings, such as sale and sail.

List Words
your
to
here
you're
too
hear

Write a List Word to complete each sentence.

1. When you whisper, I can't _____ .

2. Each person must walk _____ the exit.

3. It is getting _____ dark to read.

4. Please hang _____ coat in the hall.

5. We will be _____ when you return.

6. I see that _____ on my bus now.

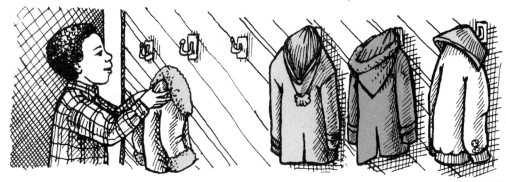

List Words

In each set of List Words, one word is misspelled. Circle the List Word that is wrong. Then write it correctly on the line.

List Words
knew
rough
unbutton
reform
couldn't
redo
wreck
disobey
refill
there's
hear
you're

1. unbutton   you're   disobay   _____
2. redoo   rough   refill   _____
3. reform   wreck   knoo   _____
4. your'e   couldn't   there's   _____
5. knew   reck   hear   _____
6. couldn't   reform   ther'es   _____
7. redo   refil   rough   _____
8. unbuton   disobey   refill   _____
9. redo   knew   heer   _____
10. wreck   rouph   you're   _____
11. disobey   refform   unbutton   _____
12. there's   you're   coudn't   _____

Go for the Goal

Take your Final Replay Test. Then fill in your Scoreboard. Send any misspelled words to your Word Locker.

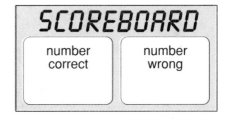

SCOREBOARD

number correct	number wrong

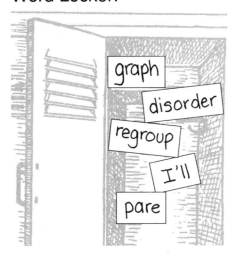

graph, disorder, regroup, I'll, pare

Clean Out Your Word Locker
Look in your Word Locker. Cross out each word you spelled correctly on your Final Replay Test. Circle the words you're still having trouble with. Add the words you circled to your Spelling Notebook. What do you notice about the words? Watch for those words as you write.

Writing and Proofreading Guide

1. Choose a topic to write about.
2. Write your ideas. Don't worry about mistakes.
3. Now organize your writing so that it makes sense.
4. Proofread your work.

    Use these proofreading marks to make changes.

	Proofreading Marks
⬯	spelling mistake
≡	capital letter
⊙	add period
∧	add something
⌄	add apostrophe
ꟼ	take out something
¶	indent paragraph
/	make small letter

did you see the ~~the~~ spider (makeng) a web?

5. Write your final copy.

    Did you see the spider making a web?

6. Share your writing.

Using Your Dictionary

The Spelling Workout Dictionary shows you
many things about your spelling words.

The **sound-spelling** or
respelling tells how
to pronounce the word.

The **entry word** listed in
alphabetical order is the
word you are looking up.

The **part of speech** is
given as an abbreviation.

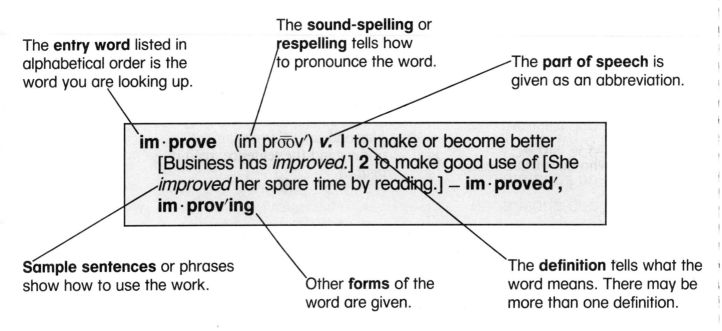

im·prove   (im proov′) **v.** I to make or become better
[Business has *improved*.] **2** to make good use of [She
improved her spare time by reading.] — **im·proved′**,
im·prov′ing

Sample sentences or phrases
show how to use the work.

Other **forms** of the
word are given.

The **definition** tells what the
word means. There may be
more than one definition.

Pronunciation Key

SYMBOL	KEY WORDS	SYMBOL	KEY WORDS	SYMBOL	KEY WORDS	SYMBOL	KEY WORDS
a	ask, fat	o͝o	look, pull	b	bed, dub	t	top, hat
ā	ape, date	o͞o	ooze, tool	d	did, had	v	vat, have
ä	car, lot	ou	out, crowd	f	fall, off	w	will, always
				g	get, dog	y	yet, yard
e	elf, ten	u	up, cut	h	he, ahead	z	zebra, haze
ē	even, meet	ʉ	fur, fern	j	joy, jump		
				k	kill, bake	ch	chin, arch
i	is, hit	ə	a in ago	l	let, ball	ŋ	ring, singer
ī	ice, fire		e in agent	m	met, trim	sh	she, dash
			e in father	n	not, ton	th	thin, truth
ō	open, go		i in unity	p	put, tap	*th*	then, father
ô	law, horn		o in collect	r	red, dear	zh	s in pleasure
oi	oil, point		u in focus	s	sell, pass		

An Americanism is a word or usage of a word that was born in this country. An open star before an
entry word or definition means that the word or definition is an Americanism.

These dictionary entries are taken, by permission, in abridged or modified form from *Webster's New World
Dictionary*. Copyright © 1992 by Simon & Schuster Inc.

a·bout (ə bout′) **adv. 1** on every side; all around [Look *about*.] **2** nearly; more or less [*about* ten years old]. ◆**adj.** active; awake or recovered [At dawn I was up and *about*.] ◆**prep. 1** almost ready [I am *about* to cry.] **2** having to do with [a book *about* ships].

ac·ro·bat (ak′rə bat) **n.** a performer who does tricks in tumbling or on the trapeze, tightrope, etc.

a·cross (ə krôs′) **adv.** from one side to the other [The new bridge makes it easy to get *across* in a car.] ◆**prep. 1** from one side to the other of [We swam *across* the river.] **2** on the other side of [They live *across* the street.]

act (akt) **n. 1** a thing done; deed [an *act* of bravery]. **2** one of the main divisions of a play, opera, etc. [The first *act* takes place in a palace.] ◆**v. 1** to play the part of, as on a stage [She *acted* Juliet.] **2** to behave like [Don't *act* the fool.]

add (ad) **v. 1** to put or join something to another thing so that there will be more or so as to mix into one thing [We *added* some books to our library. *Add* two cups of sugar to the batter.] **2** to join numbers so as to get a total, or sum [*Add* 3 and 5.]

ad·mit (əd mit′) **v. 1** to permit or give the right to enter [One ticket *admits* two persons.] **2** to take or accept as being true; confess [Lucy will not *admit* her mistake.] —**ad·mit′ted, ad·mit′ting**

ad·ver·tise (ad′vər tīz) **v. 1** to tell about a product in public and in such a way as to make people want to buy it [to *advertise* cars on television]. **2** to announce or ask for publicly, as in a newspaper [to *advertise* a house for rent; to *advertise* for a cook]. —**ad′ver·tised, ad′ver·tis·ing** —**ad′ver·tis′er n.**

af·ford (ə fôrd′) **v.** to have money enough to spare for [Can we *afford* a new car?]

af·ter·noon (af tər nōōn′) **n.** the time of day from noon to evening.

a·gain (ə gen′) **adv.** once more; a second time [If you don't understand the sentence, read it *again*.]

age (āj) **n. 1** the time that a person or thing has existed from birth or beginning [He left school at the *age* of fourteen.] **2** the fact of being old [Gray hair comes with *age*.]

air·plane (er′plān) **n.** an aircraft that is kept up by the force of air upon its wings and driven forward by a jet engine or propeller.

air·port (er′pôrt) **n.** a place where aircraft can take off and land, get fuel, or take on passengers.

a·live (ə līv′) **adj. 1** having life; living. **2** going on; in action; not ended or destroyed [to keep old memories *alive*]. **3** lively; alert.

☆**al·ler·gy** (al′ər jē) **n.** a condition in which one becomes sick, gets a rash, etc., by breathing in, touching, eating, or drinking something that is not harmful to most people [Hay fever is usually caused by an *allergy* to certain pollens.] —*pl.* **al′ler·gies**

al·low (ə lou′) **v. 1** to let be done; permit; let [*Allow* us to pay. No smoking *allowed*.] **2** to give or keep an extra amount so as to have enough [*Allow* an inch for shrinkage.]

all right 1 good enough; satisfactory; adequate [Your work is *all right*.] **2** yes; very well [*All right*, I'll do it.]

acrobat

a	ask, fat
ā	ape, date
ä	car, lot
e	elf, ten
ē	even, meet
i	is, hit
ī	ice, fire
ō	open, go
ô	law, horn
oi	oil, point
oo	look, pull
ōō	ooze, tool
ou	out, crowd
u	up, cut
ʉ	fur, fern
ə	a in ago
	e in agent
	e in father
	i in unity
	o in collect
	u in focus
ch	chin, arch
ŋ	ring, singer
sh	she, dash
th	thin, truth
th	then, father
zh	s in pleasure

al·most (ôl'mōst) *adv.* not completely but very nearly [He tripped and *almost* fell. Sue is *almost* ten.]

al·read·y (ôl red'ē) *adv.* **1** by or before this time [When we arrived, dinner had *already* begun.] **2** even now [I am *already* ten minutes late.]

al·though (ôl thō') *conj.* in spite of the fact that; even if; though [*Although* the book was very long, he enjoyed it.]

al·to·geth·er (ôl'too geth*th*ər) *adv.* to the full extent; wholly; completely [You're not *altogether* wrong.]

al·ways (ôl'wāz) *adv.* at all times; at every time [*Always* be courteous.]

an·chor (aŋ'kər) *n.* a heavy object let down into the water by a chain or rope to keep a ship or boat from drifting. ◆ *v.* to keep from drifting by using an anchor [to *anchor* the boat and go ashore].

an·gry (aŋ'grē) *adj.* **1** feeling or showing anger [*angry* words; an *angry* crowd]. **2** wild and stormy [an *angry* sea]. —**an'gri·er, an'gri·est**

an·y (en'ē) *adj.* **1** one, no matter which one, of more than two [*Any* pupil may answer.] **2** some, no matter how much, how many, or what kind [Do you have *any* apples?] ◆ *pron.* any one or ones; any amount or number [I lost my pencils; do you have *any*?]

an·y·how (en'ē hou') *adv.* **1** no matter what else may be true; in any case [I don't like the color, and *anyhow* it's not my size.] **2** no matter in what way [That's a fine report *anyhow* you look at it.]

an·y·one (en'ē wun') *pron.* any person; anybody [Does *anyone* know where the house is?]

an·y·way (en'ē wā') *adv.* nevertheless; anyhow.

Atlanta

ap·pear (ə pir') *v.* to come into sight or into being [A ship *appeared* on the horizon. Leaves *appear* on the tree every spring.]

ar·my (är'mē) *n.* **1** a large group of soldiers trained for war, especially on land; also, all the soldiers of a country. **2** any large group of persons or animals [An *army* of workers was building the bridge.] —*pl.* **ar'mies**

ash·es (ash'əz) *pl.n.* the grayish powder or fine dust that is left after something has been burned.

At·lan·ta (at lan'tə) the capital of Georgia, in the northern part.

Au·gust (ô'gəst) *n.* the eighth month of the year, which has 31 days: abbreviated **Aug.**

a·void (ə void') *v.* to keep away from; get out of the way of; shun [to *avoid* crowds].

aw·ful (ô'fəl) *adj.* **1** making one feel awe or dread; causing fear [an *awful* scene of destruction]. **2** very bad, ugly, great, etc.: *used only in everyday talk* [an *awful* joke; an *awful* fool].

awk·ward (ôk'wərd *or* äk'wərd) *adj.* not having grace or skill; clumsy; bungling [an *awkward* dancer].

aye or **ay** (ī) *adv.* yes. ◆ *n.* a vote of "yes."

ba·by (bā'bē) *n.* **1** a very young child; infant. **2** a person who seems helpless, cries easily, etc., like a baby. **3** the youngest or smallest in a group. —*pl.* **ba'bies**

bam·boo (bam boo') *n.* a tropical plant with woody stems that are hollow and jointed.

base·ment (bās'mənt) *n.* the cellar or lowest rooms of a building, below the main floor and at least partly below the surface of the ground.

be·cause (bē kôz´) **conj.** for the reason that; since [I'm late *because* I overslept.]

bed·room (bed´rōōm) **n.** a room with a bed, for sleeping in.

be·fore (bē fôr´) **prep.** earlier than; previous to [Will you finish *before* noon?] ◆**adv.** in the past; earlier [I've heard that song *before*.] ◆**conj.** earlier than the time that [Think *before* you speak.]

be·gin·ning (bē gin´iŋ) **n.** a start or starting; first part or first action [We came in just after the *beginning* of the movie. Going to the dance together was the *beginning* of our friendship.]

be·half (bē haf´) **n.** support for someone; interest [Many of his friends spoke in his *behalf*.]

be·long (bē lôŋ´) **v.** 1 to have its proper place [This chair *belongs* in the corner.] 2 to be owned by someone [This book *belongs* to you.]

be·low (bē lō´) **adv., adj.** in or to a lower place; beneath [I'll take the upper bunk and you can sleep *below*.] ◆**prep.** lower than in place, position, price, rank, etc. [the people living *below* us; a price *below* $25].

bench (bench) **n.** a long, hard seat for several persons, with or without a back.

be·neath (bē nēth´) **adv.** in a lower place; below or just below; underneath [Look *beneath* the table.] ◆**prep.** lower than; below or just below; under [the ground *beneath* my feet].

ber·ry (ber´ē) **n.** any small, juicy fruit with seeds and a soft pulp, as a strawberry, blackberry, or blueberry. In scientific use, many fleshy fruits having a skin are classed as berries, for example, the tomato, banana, and grape. —*pl.* **ber´ries**

be·side (bē sīd´) **prep.** by or at the side of; close to [The garage is *beside* the house.]

best (best) **adj.** above all others in worth or ability; most excellent, most fit, most desirable, etc. [Joan is the *best* player on the team. When is the *best* time to plant tulips?] ◆**adv.** 1 in a way that is best or most excellent, fit, etc. [Which choir sang *best*?] 2 more than any other; most [Of all your books, I like that one *best*.] ◆**n.** 1 a person or thing that is most excellent, most fit, etc. [That doctor is among the *best* in the profession. When I buy shoes, I buy the *best*.] 2 the most that can be done; utmost [We did our *best* to win.]

bet·ter (bet´ər) **adj.** 1 above another, as in worth or ability; more excellent, more fit, more desirable, etc. [Grace is a *better* player than Chris. I have a *better* idea.] 2 not so sick; more healthy than before. ◆**adv.** 1 in a way that is better or more excellent, fit, etc. [They will sing *better* with more practice.] 2 more [I like the orange drink *better* than the lime.]

big (big) **adj.** of great size; large [a *big* cake; a *big* city]. —**big´ger, big´gest** —**big´ness n.**

bird (bʉrd) **n.** a warmblooded animal that has a backbone, two feet, and wings, and is covered with feathers. Birds lay eggs and can usually fly.

bi·son (bī´sən) **n.** a wild animal that is related to the ox, with a shaggy mane, short, curved horns, and a humped back. The American bison is often called a *buffalo*. —*pl.* **bi´son**

blame (blām) **v.** to say or think that someone or something is the cause of what is wrong or bad [Don't *blame* others for your own mistakes.] —**blamed, blam´ing** ◆**n.** the fact of being the cause of what is wrong or bad [I will take the *blame* for the broken window.]

a	ask, fat
ā	ape, date
ä	car, lot
e	elf, ten
ē	even, meet
i	is, hit
ī	ice, fire
ō	open, go
ô	law, horn
oi	oil, point
ōō	look, pull
ōō	ooze, tool
ou	out, crowd
u	up, cut
ʉ	fur, fern
ə	a in ago
	e in agent
	e in father
	i in unity
	o in collect
	u in focus
ch	chin, arch
ŋ	ring, singer
sh	she, dash
th	thin, truth
th	then, father
zh	s in pleasure

blast (blast) *n.* a strong rush of air or gust of wind. ◆ *v.* to blow up with an explosive [to *blast* rock].

blaze (blāz) *n.* a bright flame or fire. ◆ *v.* to burn brightly. —**blazed, blaz'ing**

blew (blōo) *past tense of* **blow**.

blind (blīnd) *adj.* not able to see; having no sight. ◆ *v.* to make blind; make unable to see. ◆ *n.* a window shade of stiffened cloth, metal slats, etc.

blood (blud) *n.* the red liquid that is pumped through the arteries and veins by the heart. The blood carries oxygen and cell-building material to the body tissues and carries carbon dioxide and waste material away from them.

blouse (blous) *n.* a loose outer garment like a shirt, worn by women and children.

blow (blō) *v.* 1 to move with some force [There is a wind *blowing*.] 2 to force air out from the mouth [*Blow* on your hands to warm them.] —**blew, blow'ing** ◆ *n.* 1 the act of blowing. 2 a strong wind; gale.

blue (blōo) *adj.* having the color of the clear sky or the deep sea. —**blu'er, blu'est**

bod·y (bäd'ē) *n.* the whole physical part of a person or animal [Athletes have strong *bodies*.]

bot·tom (bät'əm) *n.* the lowest part [Sign your name at the *bottom* of this paper.] ◆ *adj.* of or at the bottom; lowest [the *bottom* shelf].

bought (bôt) *past tense and past participle of* **buy**.

bou·quet (bōo kā' *or* bō kā') *n.* 1 a bunch of cut flowers [a *bouquet* of roses].

branch (branch) *n.* any part of a tree growing from the trunk or from a main limb. —*pl.* **branch'es** ◆ *v.* to divide into branches [The road *branches* two miles east of town.]

break (brāk) *v.* 1 to come or make come apart by force; split or crack sharply into pieces [*Break* an egg into the bowl. The rusty hinge *broke*.] 2 to do better than; outdo [He *broke* the record for running the mile.] ◆ *n.* 1 a broken place [The X ray showed a *break* in the bone.] 2 an interruption [Recess is a relaxing *break* in our school day.]

breathe (brē*th*) *v.* to take air into the lungs and then let it out [to *breathe* deeply]. —**breathed, breath'ing**

bright (brīt) *adj.* 1 shining; giving light; full of light [a *bright* star; a *bright* day]. 2 having a quick mind; clever [a *bright* child]. —**bright'ly** *adv.* —**bright'ness** *n.*

bring (briŋ) *v.* to carry or lead here or to the place where the speaker will be [*Bring* it to my house tomorrow.] —**brought, bring'ing**

bro·ken (brō'kən) *past participle of* **break**. ◆ *adj.* 1 split or cracked into pieces [a *broken* dish; a *broken* leg]. 2 not in working condition [a *broken* watch].

brook (brook) *n.* a small stream.

broom (brōom) *n.* a brush with a long handle, used for sweeping.

brought (brôt *or* brät) *past tense and past participle of* **bring**.

brush (brush) *n.* a bunch of bristles, hairs, or wires fastened into a hard back or handle. Brushes are used for cleaning, polishing, grooming, painting, etc. —*pl.* **brush'es** ◆ *v.* 1 to use a brush on; clean, polish, paint, smooth, etc., with a brush [*Brush* your shoes. *Brush* the paint on evenly.] 2 to touch or graze in passing [The tire of the car *brushed* against the curb.]

buf·fa·lo (buf'ə lō) *n.* 1 a wild ox of Africa and Asia that is sometimes used as a work animal. 2 *another name for* the North American **bison**. —*pl.* —**buf'fa·loes** *or* **buf'fa·los** *or* **buf'fa·lo**

bunch (bunch) *n.* a group of things of the same kind growing or placed together [a *bunch* of bananas; a *bunch* of keys]. —*pl.* **bunch′es**

bush (boosh) *n.* a woody plant, smaller than a tree and having many stems branching out low instead of one main stem or trunk; shrub. —*pl.* **bush′es**

busi·ness (biz′nəs) *n.* **1** what a person does for a living; a person's work or occupation [Her *business* was writing plays.] **2** a place where things are made or sold; store or factory [Raul owns three *businesses*. — *pl.* **bus′i·ness·es**

butterfly (but′ər flī) *n.* an insect with a slender body and four broad, usually brightly colored wings. —*pl.* —**but′ter · flies**

buy (bī) *v.* to get by paying money or something else [The Dutch *bought* Manhattan Island for about $24.] —**bought, buy′ing** ◆*n.* the value of a thing compared with its price [Turnips are your best *buy* in January vegetables.]

Cc

cage (kāj) *n.* a box or closed-off space with wires or bars on the sides, in which to keep birds or animals. ◆*v.* to shut up in a cage. —**caged, cag′ing**

calf¹ (kaf) *n.* **1** a young cow or bull. **2** a young elephant, whale, hippopotamus, seal, etc. —*pl.* **calves**

calf² (kaf) *n.* the fleshy back part of the leg between the knee and the ankle. —*pl.* **calves**

camp (kamp) *n.* a place in the country where people, especially children, can have an outdoor vacation. ◆*v.* to live in a camp or in the outdoors for a time

[We'll be *camping* in Michigan this summer.]

can·dy (kan′dē) *n.* a sweet food made from sugar or syrup, with flavor, coloring, fruits, nuts, etc., added. —*pl.* **can′dies**

can·not (kan′ät *or* kə nät′) *the usual way of writing* can not.

can·vas (kan′vəs) *n.* **1** a strong, heavy cloth of hemp, cotton, or linen, used for tents, sails, or oil paintings. —*pl.* **can′vas·es**

care (ker) *n.* a watching over or tending; protection [The books were left in my *care*.] ◆*v.* **1** to watch over or take charge of something [Will you *care* for my canary while I'm gone?] **2** to feel a liking [I don't *care* for dancing.] —**cared, car′ing**

car·go (kär′gō) *n.* the load of goods carried by a ship, airplane, or truck. —*pl.* —**car′goes** or **car′gos**

car·pet (kär′pət) *n.* a thick, heavy fabric used to cover floors. ◆ *v.* to cover with a carpet or with something like a carpet [The lawn was *carpeted* with snow.]

car·ry (kar′ē) *v.* to take from one place to another; transport or conduct [Please help me *carry* these books home. The large pipe *carries* water. Air *carries* sounds.] —**car′ried, car′ry·ing**

case (kās) *n.* a container for holding and protecting something [a watch*case*; a seed*case*; a violin *case*].

catch (kach) *v.* **1** to stop by grasping with the hands or arms [to *catch* a ball]. **2** to become sick or infected with [to *catch* the flu]. —**caught, catch′ing** ◆*n.* **1** the act of catching a ball, etc. [The outfielder made a running *catch*.] **2** anything that is caught [a *catch* of 14 fish].

cat·tle (kat′l) *n.pl.* animals of the cow family that are raised on farms and ranches, as cows, bulls, steers, and oxen.

calf

a	ask, fat
ā	ape, date
ä	car, lot
e	elf, ten
ē	even, meet
i	is, hit
ī	ice, fire
ō	open, go
ô	law, horn
oi	oil, point
σσ	look, pull
ōσ	ooze, tool
ou	out, crowd
u	up, cut
ʉ	fur, fern
ə	a in ago
	e in agent
	e in father
	i in unity
	o in collect
	u in focus
ch	chin, arch
ŋ	ring, singer
sh	she, dash
th	thin, truth
th	then, father
zh	s in pleasure

caught (kôt) *past tense and past participle of* **catch.**

cent (sent) *n.* a coin worth 100th part of a dollar; penny.

chair (cher) *n.* a piece of furniture that has a back and is a seat for one person.

chalk (chôk) *n.* **1** a whitish limestone that is soft and easily crushed into a powder. It is made up mainly of tiny sea shells. **2** a piece of chalk or material like it, for writing on chalkboards.

cham·pi·on (cham′pē ən) *n.* a person, animal, or thing that wins first place or is judged to be best in a contest or sport [a spelling *champion*].

change (chānj) *v.* **1** to make or become different in some way; alter [Time *changes* all things.   His voice began to *change* at the age of thirteen.] **2** to put or take one thing in place of another; substitute [to *change* one's clothes; to *change* jobs]. —**changed, chang′ing** ◆ *n.* **1** the act of changing in some way [There will be a *change* in the weather tomorrow.] **2** something put in place of something else [a fresh *change* of clothing.] **3** the money returned when one has paid more than the amount owed [If it costs 70 cents and you pay with a dollar, you get back 30 cents as *change*.]

chap·ter (chap′tər) *n.* any of the main parts into which a book is divided.

chart (chärt) *n.* **1** a map, especially one for use in steering a ship or guiding an aircraft [A sailor's *chart* shows coastlines, depths, currents, etc.] **2** a group of facts about something set up in the form of a diagram, graph, table, etc. ◆ *v.* to make a map of.

chase (chās) *v.* to go after or keep following in order to catch or harm [The fox was *chasing* a rabbit.] —**chased, chas′ing**

chart

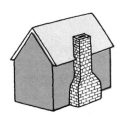

chimney

cheap (chēp) *adj.* low in price [Vegetables are *cheaper* in summer than in winter.] ◆ *adv.* at a low cost [I bought these shoes *cheap* at a sale.] —**cheap′ly** *adv.* —**cheap′ness** *n.*

check (chek) *n.* **1** the mark √, used to show that something is right or to call attention to something. **2** a written order to a bank to pay a certain amount of money from one's account to a certain person. ◆ *v.* ☆to prove to be right or find what is wanted by examining, comparing, etc. [These figures *check* with mine.   *Check* the records for this information.]

cheer (chir) *n.* **1** a glad, excited shout of welcome, joy, or approval [The crowd gave the team three *cheers*.] **2** good or glad feelings; joy, hope, etc. [a visit that brought *cheer* to the invalid]. ◆ *v.* **1** to make or become glad or hopeful [Things are getting better, so *cheer* up!] **2** to urge on or applaud with cheers.

chew·y (chōō′ē) *adj.* needing much chewing [*chewy* candy]. —**chew′i·er, chew′i·est**

child (chīld) *n.* **1** a baby; infant. **2** a young boy or girl. **3** a son or daughter [Their *children* are all grown up.] —*pl.* **chil′dren**

chil·dren (chil′drən) *n.* *plural of* **child.**

chim·ney (chim′nē) *n.* a pipe or shaft going up through a roof to carry off smoke from a furnace, fireplace, or stove. Chimneys are usually enclosed with brick or stone. —*pl.* **chim′neys**

choice (chois) *n.* **1** the act of choosing or picking; selection [You may have a dessert of your own *choice*.] **2** a person or thing chosen [Green is my *choice* for mayor.] —**choic′er, choic′est**

choose (chōōz) *v.* to pick out one or more from a number or group [*Choose* a subject from this list.] —**chose, cho′sen, choos′ing**

chop (chäp) *v.* **1** to cut by strokes with a sharp tool [to *chop* down a tree]. —**chopped, chop′ping**

churn (chʉrn) *n.* a container in which milk or cream is stirred hard or shaken to make butter. ◆ *v.* to use a churn to make butter [to *churn* milk or cream].

cir·cus (sʉr′kəs) *n.* a traveling show held in tents or in a hall, with clowns, trained animals, acrobats, etc.

clap (klap) *v.* to make a sudden, loud sound like that of two flat surfaces being struck together [I *clapped* my hands.] —**clapped, clap′ping**

class (klas) *n.* ☆a group of students meeting together to be taught; also, a meeting of this kind [My English *class* is held at 9 o'clock.] —*pl.* **class′es**

clean (klēn) *adj.* **1** without dirt or impure matter [*clean* dishes; *clean* oil]. **2** neat and tidy [to keep a *clean* desk]. ◆ *v.* to make clean. [Please *clean* the oven.]

clear (klir) *adj.* **1** bright or sunny; without clouds or mist [a *clear* day]. **2** that can be seen through; transparent [*clear* glass]. **3** without anything in the way; not blocked; open [a *clear* view; a *clear* passage]. ◆ *adv.* in a clear manner; clearly [The bells rang out *clear*.] ◆ *v.* to empty or remove [*Clear* the snow from the sidewalk. Help me *clear* the table of dishes.] —**clear′ly adv.** —**clear′ness n.**

climb (klīm) *v.* to go up, or sometimes down, by using the feet and often the hands [to *climb* the stairs; to *climb* up or down a tree]. ◆ *n.* the act of climbing; rise; ascent [a tiring *climb*]. —**climb′er n.**

close (klōs) *adj.* **1** with not much space between; near [The old houses are too *close* to each other.] **2** thorough or careful [Pay *close* attention.] —**clos′er, clos′est** ◆ *adv.* so as to be close or near; closely [Follow *close* behind the leader.] —**close′ly adv.** —**close′ness n.**

clown (kloun) *n.* **1** a person who entertains, as in a circus, by doing comical tricks and silly stunts; jester; buffoon. **2** a person who likes to make jokes or act in a comical way [the *clown* of our family].

clue (klōō) *n.* a fact or thing that helps to solve a puzzle or mystery [Muddy footprints were a *clue* to the man's guilt.]

coach (kōch) *n.* **1** a large, closed carriage drawn by horses, with the driver's seat outside. **2** a person who teaches and trains students, athletes, singers, and so on. ◆ *v.* to teach, train, or tutor [Will you *coach* me for the test in history?]

cock·er spaniel (käk′ər) a small dog with long, drooping ears, long, silky hair, and short legs.

coin (koin) *n.* a piece of metal money having a certain value.

col·lar (käl′ər) *n.* **1** the part of a garment that fits around the neck. It is sometimes a separate piece or a band that is folded over. **2** the part of a horse's harness that fits around its neck.

com·ma (käm′ə) *n.* a punctuation mark (,) used to show a pause that is shorter than the pause at the end of a sentence [The *comma* is often used between clauses or after the opening phrase of a sentence. Words, numbers, or phrases in a series are separated by *commas*.]

a	ask, fat
ā	ape, date
ä	car, lot
e	elf, ten
ē	even, meet
i	is, hit
ī	ice, fire
ō	open, go
ô	law, horn
oi	oil, point
͏oo	look, pull
o͞o	ooze, tool
ou	out, crowd
u	up, cut
ʉ	fur, fern
ə	a in ago
	e in agent
	e in father
	i in unity
	o in collect
	u in focus
ch	chin, arch
ŋ	ring, singer
sh	she, dash
th	thin, truth
th	then, father
zh	s in pleasure

157

cooler

crown

com·pare (kəm per′) **v.** **1** to describe as being the same; liken [The sound of thunder can be *compared* to the roll of drums.] **2** to examine certain things in order to find out how they are alike or different [How do the two cars *compare* in size and price?] —**com·pared′, com·par′ing**

cone (kōn) **n.** **1** a solid object that narrows evenly from a flat circle at one end to a point at the other. **2** anything shaped like this, as a shell of pastry for holding ice cream. **3** the fruit of some evergreen trees, containing the seeds.

con·tain (kən tān′) **v.** to have in it; hold; enclose or include [This bottle *contains* cream. Your list *contains* 25 names.]

cook·ie or **cook·y** (kook′ē) **n.** ☆a small, flat, sweet cake. —*pl.* **cook′ies**

cool·er (kool′ər) **n.** a container or room in which things are cooled or kept cool.

cop·y (käp′ē) **n.** **1** a thing made just like another; imitation or likeness [four carbon *copies* of a letter]. **2** any one of a number of books, magazines, pictures, etc., with the same printed matter [a library with six *copies* of *Tom Sawyer*]. —*pl.* **cop′ies** ◆v. **1** to make a copy or copies of [*Copy* the questions that are on the chalkboard.] **2** to act or be the same as; imitate. —**cop′ied, cop′y·ing**

cor·ne·a (kôr′nē ə) **n.** the clear outer layer of the eyeball, covering the iris and the pupil.

cost (kôst) **v.** to be priced at; be sold for [It *costs* a dime.] —**cost, cost′ing** ◆n. amount of money, time, work, etc., asked or paid for something; price [the high *cost* of meat].

cough (kôf) **v.** **1** to force air from the lungs with a sudden, loud noise, as to clear the throat.

2 to get out of the throat by coughing [to *cough* up phlegm]. ◆n. a condition of coughing often [I have a bad *cough*.]

could·n't (kood′nt) could not.

coun·try (kun′trē) **n.** **1** an area of land; region [wooded *country*]. **2** the whole land of a nation [The *country* of Japan is made up of islands.] **3** land with farms and small towns; land outside of cities [Let's drive out to the *country*.] —*pl.* **coun′tries**

crack (krak) **v.** to break or split, with or without the parts falling apart [The snowball *cracked* the window.]◆n. a break, usually with the parts stilll holding together [a *crack* in a cup].

crawl (krôl) **v.** to move slowly by dragging the body along the ground as a worm does. ◆n. a crawling; slow, creeping movement.

cra·zy (krā′zē) **adj.** **1** mentally ill; insane. **2** very foolish or mad [a *crazy* idea]. —**cra′zi·er, cra′zi·est** —**cra′zi·ly adv.** —**cra′zi·ness n.**

creek (krēk *or* krik) **n.** a small stream, a little larger than a brook.

crib (krib) **n.** a small bed with high sides, for a baby.

cricket (krik′it) **n.** a leaping insect related to the grasshopper.

crook·ed (krook′əd) **adj.** **1** not straight; bent, curved, or twisted [a *crooked* road]. **2** not honest; cheating.

crowd (kroud) **n.** a large group of people together [*crowds* of Christmas shoppers]. ◆v. to push or squeeze [Can we all *crowd* into one car?]

crown (kroun) **n.** a headdress of gold, jewels, etc., worn by a king or queen. ◆v. to make a king or queen by putting a crown on [Elizabeth I was *crowned* in 1558.]

cut (kut) *v.* **1** to make an opening in with a knife or other sharp tool; pierce; gash [Andy *cut* his chin while shaving.] **2** to divide into parts with such a tool; sever [Will you *cut* the cake?] **3** to make shorter by trimming [to *cut* one's hair]. **4** to go through or across, usually to make a shorter way [The path *cuts* across the meadow. The tunnel *cuts* through the mountain.] —**cut, cut′ting**

Dd

Dal·las (dal′əs) a city in northeastern Texas.

Dal·ma·tian (dal mā′shən) *n.* a large dog with short hair and a black-and-white coat.

dance (dans) *v.* to move the body and feet in some kind of rhythm, usually to music [to *dance* a waltz or a minuet]. —**danced, danc′ing**

dan·ger (dān′jər) *n.* **1** a condition in which there could be harm, trouble, loss, etc.; risk; peril [to live in constant *danger*].

dark (därk) *adj.* having little or no light [a *dark* night]. — **dark′ness** *n.*

dash (dash) *v.* to move quickly; rush [The thief *dashed* down the alley.] ✦*n.* **1** a little bit; pinch [Put a *dash* of salt in the salad.] ☆**2** a short, fast run or race [a 100-yard *dash*]. **3** the mark (—), used in printing or writing.

dead (ded) *adj.* no longer living; without life [Throw out those *dead* flowers.] ✦*adv.* completely; entirely [I am *dead* tired from running.] ✦*n.* the time of most cold, most darkness, etc. [the *dead* of winter; the *dead* of night].

deer (dir) *n.* a swift-running, hoofed animal that chews its cud. The male usually has antlers that are shed every year. —*pl.* **deer.**

de·pend (dē pend′) *v.* **1** to be controlled or decided by [The attendance at the game *depends* on the weather.] **2** to put one's trust in; be sure of [You can't *depend* on this weather.] **3** to rely on for help or support [They *depend* on their parents for money.]

desk (desk) *n.* a piece of furniture with a smooth top at which one can write, draw, or read. It often has drawers for storing things.

des·sert (də zurt′) *n.* something sweet served at the end of a meal.

de·stroy (dē stroi′) *v.* to put an end to by breaking up, tearing down, ruining, or spoiling [The flood *destroyed* 300 homes.]

de·vice (dē vīs′) *n.* something made or invented for some special use. [A windmill is a *device* for putting wind power to work.]

did·n't (did′nt) did not.

dig (dig) *v.* **1** to turn up or remove ground with a spade, the hands, claws, etc. [The children are *digging* in the sand.] **2** to make by digging [to *dig* a well]. —**dug** *or in older use* **digged, dig′ging**

dim (dim) *adj.* not bright or clear; somewhat dark; shadowy; gloomy [the *dim* twilight]. — **dim′mer, dim′mest**

dis·ap·pear (dis ə pir′) *v.* to stop being seen or to stop existing; vanish [The car *disappeared* around a curve. Dinosaurs *disappeared* millions of years ago.] —**dis′ap·pear′ance** *n.*

dis·cov·er (dis kuv′ər) *v.* to be the first to find, see, or learn about [Marie and Pierre Curie *discovered* radium.]

dish (dish) *n.* any of the plates, bowls, saucers, etc., used to serve food at the table. —*pl.* **dish′es** ✦ *v.* to serve in a dish [*Dish* up the beans.] —**dish′ful** *adj.*

desk

a	ask, fat
ā	ape, date
ä	car, lot
e	elf, ten
ē	even, meet
i	is, hit
ī	ice, fire
ō	open, go
ô	law, horn
oi	oil, point
͡oo	look, pull
͞oo	ooze, tool
ou	out, crowd
u	up, cut
u	fur, fern
ə	a in ago
	e in agent
	e in father
	i in unity
	o in collect
	u in focus
ch	chin, arch
ŋ	ring, singer
sh	she, dash
th	thin, truth
th	then, father
zh	s in pleasure

ditch

dis·like (dis līk′) **v.** to have a feeling of not liking; be opposed to [I *dislike* people I can't trust.] —**dis·liked′, dis·lik′ing** ◆**n.** a feeling of not liking; distaste [The gardener felt a strong *dislike* for toads.]

dis·o·bey (dis′ ō bā′) **v.** to fail to obey or refuse to obey.

dis·or·der (dis ôr′dər) **n.** lack of order; jumble; confusion [The troops retreated in *disorder.*]

dis·please (dis plēz′) **v.** to make angry or not satisfied; annoy. —**dis·pleased′, dis·pleas′ing**

dis·re·spect (dis′rē spekt′) **n.** lack of respect or politeness; rudeness.—**dis′re·spect′ful adj.** —**dis′re·spect′ful·ly adv.**

dis·taste (dis tāst′) **n.** dislike; aversion [a *distaste* for worms].

dis·trust (dis trust′) **n.** a lack of trust; doubt; suspicion. ◆**v.** to have no trust in; doubt. —**dis·trust′ful adj.**

ditch (dich) **n.** a long, narrow opening dug in the earth, as for carrying off water; trench [a *ditch* along the road].

do (dōō) **v. 1** to work at or carry out an action; perform [What do you *do* for a living? I'll *do* the job.] **2** to bring about; cause [The storm *did* a lot of damage.] **3** to put forth; exert [She *did* her best.] **4** to take care of; attend to [Who will *do* the dishes?] —**did, done, do′ing**

does (duz) *the form of the verb* **do** *showing the present time with singular nouns and with* he, she, *or* it.

does·n't (duz′nt) does not.

don't (dōnt) do not.

doubt (dout) **v. 1** to think that something may not be true or right; be unsure of; question [I *doubt* that this is the correct answer.] **2** to consider unlikely [I *doubt* it will snow today.] ′ **n.** a feeling of not being sure or certain of [I have no *doubt* that you will return safely.]

drain (drān) **v.** to make flow away [*Drain* the water from the potatoes.] ′ **n.** a pipe or channel for carrying off water [a bathtub *drain*].

dress·ing (dres′iŋ) **n. 1** a bandage or medicine for a wound or sore. **2** a sauce, as of oil, vinegar, and seasoning, added to salads and other dishes. **3** a stuffing, as of bread and seasoning, for roast chicken, turkey, etc.

drive (drīv) **v.** to control the movement of an automobile, horse and wagon, bus, etc. —**drove, driv′en, driv′ing** ◆**n. 1** a trip in an automobile, etc. **2** a street, road, or driveway.

drove (drōv) *past tense of* **drive.**

drown (droun) **v.** to die from being under water, where the lungs can get no air [to fall overboard and *drown*].

dry (drī) **adj. 1** not wet or damp; without moisture. **2** having little or no rain or water [a *dry* summer]. **3** thirsty. —**dri′er, dri′est** ◆**v.** to make or become dry. —**dried, dry′ing** —**dry′ly adv.** —**dry′ness n.**

dug (dug) *past tense and past participle of* **dig.**

each (ēch) **adj., pron.** every one of two or more, thought of separately [*Each* pupil will receive a book. *Each* of the books is numbered.] ◆**adv.** for each; apiece [Tickets cost $5.00 *each*.]

ea·ger (ē′gər) **adj.** wanting very much; anxious to do or get [*eager* to win; *eager* for praise]. —**ea′ger·ly adv.** —**ea′ger·ness n.**

ear·ly (ur'lē) *adv., adj.* **1** near the beginning; soon after the start [in the *early* afternoon; *early* in his career]. **2** before the usual or expected time [The bus arrived *early*.] —**ear'li·er, ear'li·est** —**ear'li·ness** *n.*

earn (urn) *v.* **1** to get as pay for work done [She *earns* $10 an hour.] **2** to get or deserve because of something one has done [At the Olympics she *earned* a gold medal for swimming.]

earth (urth) *n.* **1** the planet that we live on. It is the fifth largest planet and the third in distance away from the sun. **2** the dry part of the earth's surface, that is not the sea. **3** soil or ground [a flowerpot filled with good, rich *earth*].

east (ēst) *n.* **1** the direction toward the point where the sun rises. **2** a place or region in or toward this direction. ◆*adj.* in, of, to, or toward the east [the *east* bank of the river]. ◆*adv.* in or toward the east [Go *east* ten miles.]

eas·y (ē'zē) *adj.* not hard to do, learn or get [an *easy* job]. —'eas'i·er, eas'i·est

egg (eg) *n.* the oval or round body that is laid by a female bird, fish, reptile, insect, etc., and from which a young bird, fish, etc., is later hatched. It has a brittle shell or tough outer skin.

eight (āt) *n., adj.* one more thn seven; the number 8.

el·e·phant (el'ə fənt) *n.* a huge animal with a thick skin, two ivory tusks, and a long snout, or trunk. It is found in Africa and India and is the largest of the four-legged animals.

else (els) *adj.* **1** not the same; different; other [I thought you were someone *else*.] **2** that may be added; more [Do you want anything *else*?] ◆*adv.* in a different time, place, or way [Where *else* did you go?]

emp·ty (emp'tē) *adj.* having nothing or no one in it; not occupied; vacant [an *empty* jar; an *empty* house]. —**emp'ti·er, emp'ti·est** ◆*v.* to take out or pour out [*Empty* the dirty water in the sink.] —**emp'tied, emp'ty·ing** —*pl.* **emp'ties** —**emp'ti·ly** *adv.* —**emp'ti·ness** *n.*

en·joy (en joi') *v.* to get joy or pleasure from [We *enjoyed* the baseball game.]

e·rase (ē rās') *v.* to rub out; scrape away [to *erase* writing].

ev·er·y (ev'rē) *adj.* **1** all the group of which the thing named is one; each [*Every* student must take the test. She has read *every* book on the list.] **2** all that there could be [You've been given *every* chance.]

ev·er·y·bod·y (ev'rē bäd'e *or* ev'rē bud'ē) *pron.* every person; everyone [*Everybody* loves a good story.]

ev·er·y·where (ev'rē hwer) *adv.* in or to every place [*Everywhere* I go I meet friends.]

ex·er·cise (ek'sər sīz) *n.* the active use of the body in order to make it stronger or healthier [Long walks are good outdoor *exercise*.] ◆*v.* to put into use or do certain regular movements, in order to develop or train [I *exercise* every morning.]

eye (ī) *n.* the part of the body with which a human being or animal sees. ◆*v.* to look at; observe [We *eyed* the stranger suspiciously.] —**eyed, ey'ing**

elephant

face (fās) *n.* the front part of the head, including the eyes, nose, and mouth. ◆*v.* to turn toward or have the face turned toward [Please *face* the class. Our house *faces* a park.] —**faced, fac'ing**

a	ask, fat
ā	ape, date
ä	car, lot
e	elf, ten
ē	even, meet
i	is, hit
ī	ice, fire
ō	open, go
ô	law, horn
oi	oil, point
ōō	look, pull
o͞o	ooze, tool
ou	out, crowd
u	up, cut
u	fur, fern
ə	a in ago
	e in agent
	e in father
	i in unity
	o in collect
	u in focus
ch	chin, arch
ŋ	ring, singer
sh	she, dash
th	thin, truth
th	then, father
zh	s in pleasure

fail (fāl) *v.* **1** to not do what one tried to do or what one should have done; not succeed; miss or neglect [She *failed* as a singer. He *failed* to keep his promise.] **2** to give or get a grade that shows one has not passed a test, a school course, etc.

fam·i·ly (fam'ə lē) *n.* **1** a group made up of two parents and all of their children. **2** a group of people who are related by marriage or a common ancestor; relatives; clan. —*pl.* **fam'i·lies**

farm·er (fär'mər) *n.* a person who owns or works on a farm.

fast¹ (fast) *adj.* moving, working, etc., at high speed; rapid; quick; swift [a *fast* pace; a *fast* reader]. ◆*adv.* **1** at a high speed; swiftly; rapidly [arrested for driving too *fast*]. **2** in a complete way; soundly; thoroughly [*fast* asleep].

fast² (fast) *v.* to go without any food or certain foods, as in following the rules of one's religion.

fear (fir) *n.* the feeling one has when danger, pain, or trouble is near; feeling of being worried or excited or of wanting to run and hide [Jungle animals have a natural *fear* of lions.] ◆*v.* to feel fear of; be afraid of; dread [Even brave people can *fear* real danger.]

feast (fēst) *n.* a large meal with many courses; banquet. ◆*v.* to eat a big or rich meal.

feel (fēl) *v.* **1** to touch in order to find out something [*Feel* the baby's bottle to see if the milk is warm.] **2** to be aware of through the senses or the mind [He *felt* rain on his face. Do you *feel* pain in this tooth?] **3** to think or believe [She *feels* that we should go.] —**felt, feel'ing** ◆*n.* the way a thing feels to the touch [It seems to be all wool by the *feel* of it.]

felt¹ (felt) *n.* a heavy material made of wool, fur, or hair pressed together under heat. ◆*adj.* made of felt [a *felt* hat].

felt² (felt) *past tense and past participle of* **feel**.

fifth (fifth) *adj.* coming after four others; 5th in order. ◆*n.* one of five equal parts of something; 1/5.

fight (fīt) *v.* to use fists, weapons, or other force in trying to beat or overcome someone or something; battle; struggle [to *fight* hand to hand; to *fight* a war]. —**fought, fight'ing** ◆*n.* the use of force to beat or overcome someone or something; battle.

fin·ish (fin'ish) *v.* to bring or come to an end; complete or become completed [Did you *finish* your work? The game *finished* early.] ◆*n.* **1** the last part; end [The audience stayed to the *finish*.] **2** the kind of surface a thing has [an oil *finish* on wood]. —**fin'ished** *adj.*

first (furst) *adj.* before another or before all others in time, order, quality, etc.; earliest, foremost, etc. [the *first* snow of winter; the *first* door to the right; *first* prize]. ◆*adv.* before anything or anyone else [*First* we had soup. Guests are served *first*.] ◆*n.* **1** the one that is first [to be the *first* to succeed]. **2** the beginning; start [At *first*, I believed him.]

fish (fish) *n.* an animal that lives in water and has a backbone, fins, and gills for breathing. Most fish are covered with scales. —*pl.* **fish** (or when different kinds are meant, **fishes**) [She caught three *fish*. The aquarium exhibits many *fishes*.] ◆*v.* to catch or try to catch fish.

flaw (flô) *n.* a break, scratch, crack, etc., that spoils something; blemish [There is a *flaw* in this diamond.] —**flaw'less** *adj.* —**flaw'less·ly** *adv.*

flex (fleks) *v.* **1** to bend [to *flex* an arm]. **2** to make tighter and harder; contract [to *flex* a muscle].

flight (flīt) **n.** **1** the act or way of flying or moving through space [the swift *flight* of birds]. **2** a trip through the air [a long *flight* from Los Angeles to New York].

float (flōt) **v.** **1** to rest on top of water or other liquid and not sink [Ice *floats.*] **2** to move or drift slowly, as on a liquid or through the air [Clouds *floated* overhead.] ◆**n.** a platform on wheels that carries a display or exhibit in a parade. —**float′er n.**

flood (flud) **n.** an overflowing of water onto a place that is usually dry. ◆**v.** to flow over its banks onto nearby land [The river *floods* every spring.]

floor (flôr) **n.** the bottom part of a room, hall, etc., on which to walk.

flow·er (flou′ər) **n.** the part of a plant that bears the seed and usually has brightly colored petals; blossom or bloom. ◆**v.** to come into bloom; bear flowers.

fly[1] (flī) **v.** **1** to move through the air by using wings, as a bird. **2** to travel or carry through the air, as in an aircraft. —**flew, flown, fly′ing**

fly[2] (flī) **n.** **1** a flying insect having one pair of wings, as the housefly and gnat. —*pl.* **flies**

fog (fôg *or* fäg) **n.** **1** a large mass of tiny drops of water, near the earth's surface; thick mist that makes it hard to see. **2** a condition of being confused or bewildered. —**fogged, fog′ging**

fog·gy (fôg′ē *or* fäg′ē) **adj.** **1** having fog [a *foggy* day]. **2** mixed up; confused [a *foggy* idea]. —**fog′gi·er, fog′gi·est** —**fog′gi·ly adv.** —**fog′gi·ness n.**

foil[1] (foil) **v.** to keep from doing something; thwart; stop [Their evil plans were *foiled* again.]

foil[2] (foil) **n.** a very thin sheet of metal [aluminum *foil*].

fold (fōld) **v.** to bend something over upon itself so that one part is on top of another [You *fold* a letter before putting it in an envelope.]

for·est (fôr′əst) **n.** many trees growing closely together over a large piece of land; large woods. ◆**v.** to plant with trees.

fork (fôrk) **n.** **1** a tool with a handle at one end and two or more points or prongs at the other, used to pick up something. Small forks are used in eating, and large forks, as pitchforks, are used for tossing hay and manure on a farm. ☆**2** the point where something divides into two or more branches [the *fork* of a road or of a tree]. ◆**v.** to divide into branches [Go left where the road *forks.*]

for·ward (fôr′wərd) **adj.** at, toward, or of the front [the *forward* part]. ◆**adv.** to the front; ahead [We moved slowly *forward* in the ticket line.]

fought (fôt) *past tense and past participle of* **fight**.

four (fôr) **n., adj.** one more than three; the number 4.

fourth (fôrth) **adj.** coming after three others; 4th in order. ◆**n.** one of four equal parts of something; 1/4.

frame (frām) **n.** **1** the support or skeleton around which a thing is built and that gives the thing its shape; framework [the *frame* of a house]. **2** the border or case into which a window, door, picture, etc., is set. ◆**v.** **1** to put a frame, or border, around [to *frame* a picture]. ☆**2** to make an innocent person seem guilty by a plot: *used only in everyday talk.* —**framed, fram′ing**

frame

a	ask, fat
ā	ape, date
ä	car, lot
e	elf, ten
ē	even, meet
i	is, hit
ī	ice, fire
ō	open, go
ô	law, horn
oi	oil, point
ŏŏ	look, pull
ōō	ooze, tool
ou	out, crowd
u	up, cut
ʉ	fur, fern
ə	a in ago
	e in agent
	e in father
	i in unity
	o in collect
	u in focus
ch	chin, arch
ŋ	ring, singer
sh	she, dash
th	thin, truth
th	then, father
zh	s in pleasure

163

free (frē) *adj.* **1** not under the control of another; not a slave or not in prison. **2** able to vote and to speak, write, meet, and worship as one pleases; having political and civil liberty. **3** not tied up, fastened, or shut in; loose [As soon as the bird was *free*, it flew away.] **4** with no charge; without cost [*free* tickets to the ball game]. —**fre′er, fre′est** ◆ *v.* to make free [The governor *freed* five prisoners by granting pardons.] —**freed, free′ing.**

freeze (frēz) *v.* to harden into ice; make or become solid because of cold [Water *freezes* at 0°C or 32°F.] —**froze, freez′ing**

freight (frāt) *n.* a load of goods shipped by train, truck, ship, or airplane.

fresh (fresh) *adj.* **1** newly made, got, or grown; not spoiled, stale, etc. [*fresh* coffee; *fresh* eggs]. **2** cool and clean [*fresh* air]. —**fresh′ly** *adv.* —**fresh′ness** *n.*

Fri·day (frī′dā) *n.* the sixth day of the week.

friend (frend) *n.* a person whom one knows well and likes.

fright (frīt) *n.* **1** sudden fear; alarm. **2** something that looks so strange or ugly as to startle one [That old fur coat is a perfect *fright.*]

frost (frôst) *n.* **1** frozen dew or vapor in the form of white crystals [the *frost* on the ground]. **2** cold weather that can freeze things [*Frost* in the spring may damage fruit trees.]

frown (froun) *v.* to wrinkle the forehead and draw the eyebrows together in anger, worry, or deep thought. ◆ *n.* a frowning or the look one has in frowning.

fro·zen (frōz′ən) *past participle of* **freeze.** ◆ *adj.* turned into or covered with ice [a *frozen* pond].

fry (frī) *v.* to cook in hot fat over direct heat [to *fry* eggs]. —**fried, fry′ing**

fume (fyōōm) *n. often* **fumes,** *pl.* a gas, smoke, or vapor, especially if harmful or bad-smelling. ◆ *v.* **1** to give off fumes. **2** to show that one is angry or irritated [He *fumed* at the long delay.] —**fumed, fum′ing**

Gg

garage (gər äzh′ *or* gər äj′′) *n.* **1** a closed place where automobiles are sheltered. **2** a place where automobiles are repaired.

gar·den (gärd′n) *n.* a piece of ground where flowers, vegetables, etc., are grown. ◆ *v.* to take care of a garden. —**gar·den·er** (gärd′nər) *n.*

gaze (gāz) *v.* to look in a steady way; stare [The crowd *gazed* in wonder at the spaceship.] —**gazed, gaz′ing**

geese (gēs) *n. plural of* **goose.**

gi·ant (jī′ənt) *n.* **1** an imaginary being that looks like a person but is many times larger and stronger. **2** a person or thing that is especially large, strong, etc. [Einstein was a mental *giant.*]

give (giv) *v.* **1** to pass or hand over to another [*Give* me your coat and I'll hang it up.] **2** to hand over to another to keep; make a gift of [My uncle *gave* a book to me for my birthday.] —**gave, giv′en, giv′ing** —**giv′er** *n.*

glaze (glāz) *v.* **1** to give a hard, shiny finish to [to *glaze* pottery]. **2** to cover with a sugar coating [to *glaze* doughnuts]. —**glazed, glaz′ing**

glide (glīd) *v.* to move along in a smooth and easy way [Skaters *glided* across the ice.] —**glid′ed, glid′ing**

glis·ten (glis′ən) *v.* to shine or sparkle with reflected light [The snow *glistened* in the sunlight.]

gloom·y (glōōm′ē) *adj.* **1** dark or dim [a *gloomy* dungeon]. **2** having or giving a feeling of deep sadness [a *gloomy* story]. —**gloom′i·er, gloom′i·est**

glue (glōō) *n.* **1** a thick, sticky substance made by boiling animal hoofs and bones, used for sticking things together. **2** any sticky substance like this. ◆*v.* to stick together with glue. —**glued, glu′ing** —**glue′y** *adj.*

gob·ble[1] (gäb′əl) *n.* the throaty sound made by a male turkey. ◆*v.* to make this sound. —**gob′bled, gob′bling**

gob·ble[2] (gäb′əl) *v.* to eat quickly and greedily. —**gob′bled, gob′bling**

gone (gôn) *past participle of* **go**. ◆*adj.* **1** moved away; departed. **2** used up.

good·bye or **good-bye** (good bī′) *interj., n.* a word said when leaving someone; farewell [We said our *goodbyes* quickly and left.] —*pl.* **good·byes′** or **good-byes′**

good·ness (good′nəs) *n.* the condition of being good. ◆*interj.* an exclamation showing surprise [My *goodness! Goodness* me!]

goose (gōōs) *n.* a swimming bird that is like a duck but has a larger body and a longer neck; especially, the female of this bird.— *pl.* **geese**

graph (graf) *n.* a chart or diagram that shows the changes taking place in something, by the use of connected lines, a curve, etc. [a *graph* showing how sales figures vary during the year].

grate[1] (grāt) *v.* to grind into small bits or shreds by rubbing against a rough surface [to *grate* cabbage]. —**grat′ed, grat′ing**

grate[2] (grāt) *n.* **1** a frame of metal bars for holding fuel, as in a fireplace or furnace. **2** a framework of bars set in a window or door; grating.

great (grāt) *adj.* **1** much above the average in size, degree, power, etc.; big or very big; much or very much [the *Great* Lakes; a *great* distance; *great* pain]. **2** very important; noted; remarkable [a *great* composer; a *great* discovery]. **3** older or younger by a generation: *used in words formed with a hyphen* [my *great*-aunt; my *great*-niece]. —**great′ly** *adv.* —**great′ness** *n.*

grind (grīnd) *v.* **1** to crush into tiny bits or into powder [The miller *grinds* grain between millstones.] **2** to sharpen or smooth by rubbing against a rough surface [to *grind* a knife]. **3** to press down or rub together harshly or with a grating sound [She *ground* her teeth in anger.] —**ground, grind′ing**

ground[1] (ground) *n.* the solid part of the earth's surface; land; earth. ◆*adj.* of, on, or near the ground [the *ground* floor of a building].

ground[2] (ground) *past tense and past participle of* **grind**.

group (grōōp) *n.* a number of persons or things gathered together. ◆*v.* to gather together into a group [*Group* yourselves in a circle.]

Monthly Sales (in thousands of dollars)

graph

half (haf) *n.* either of the two equal parts of something [Five is *half* of ten.] —*pl.* **halves** ◆*adj.* being either of the two equal parts [a *half* gallon].

harm (härm) *n.* **1** damage or hurt [Too much rain can do *harm* to crops.] **2** wrong; evil [I meant no *harm* by my remark.] ◆*v.* to do harm to; hurt or damage [Some cleaning fluids can *harm* the skin.]

a	ask, fat
ā	ape, date
ä	car, lot
e	elf, ten
ē	even, meet
i	is, hit
ī	ice, fire
ō	open, go
ô	law, horn
oi	oil, point
oo	look, pull
ōō	ooze, tool
ou	out, crowd
u	up, cut
u	fur, fern
ə	a in ago
	e in agent
	e in father
	i in unity
	o in collect
	u in focus
ch	chin, arch
ŋ	ring, singer
sh	she, dash
th	thin, truth
th	then, father
zh	s in pleasure

has·n't (haz'ənt) has not.

hatch (hach) **v.** to come forth from the egg [Our chicks *hatched* this morning.]

haul (hôl) **v. 1** to move by pulling; drag or tug [We *hauled* the boat up on the beach.] **2** to carry by wagon, truck, etc. [He *hauls* steel for a large company.] ◆**n.** the distance that something is hauled [It's a long *haul* to town.]

have·n't (hav'ənt) have not.

health (helth) **n.** the condition of being well in body and mind; freedom from sickness.

hear (hir) **v. 1** to receive sound through the ears [I *hear* music. Pat doesn't *hear* well.] **2** to listen to; pay attention [*Hear* what I tell you.] —**heard** (hurd), **hear′ing**

heav·y (hev'ē) **adj.** hard to lift or move because of its weight; weighing very much [a *heavy* load]. —**heav′i·er, heav′i·est** —**heav′i·ly adv.** —**heav′i·ness n.**

hel·lo (he lō') **interj.** a word used in greeting someone or in answering the telephone. ◆**n.** a saying or calling of "hello." —*pl.* **hel·los′** ◆**v.** to say or call "hello." —**hel·loed′, hel·lo′ing**

help (help) **v. 1** to give or do something that is needed or useful; make things easier for; aid; assist [We *helped* our poor relatives. *Help* me lift this.] **2** to make better; give relief to; remedy [This medicine will *help* your cold.] ◆**n.** the act of helping or a thing that helps; aid; assistance [Your advice was a great *help*.] —**help′er n.**

here (hir) **adv.** at or in this place [Who lives *here*?] ◆**interj.** a word called out to get attention, answer a roll call, etc. ◆**n.** this place [Let's get out of *here*.]

he·ro (hir'ō) **n. 1** a person, especially a man or boy, who is looked up to for having done something brave or noble [He became a *hero* when he saved his family from a burning house. Washington was the *hero* of the American Revolution.] **2** the most important man in a novel, play, etc., especially if he is good or noble. —*pl.* **he′roes**

he's (hēz) **1** he is. **2** he has.

high·way (hī'wā) **n.** a main road.

hock·ey (häk'ē) **n.** a game played on ice, in which the players wear ice skates and use curved sticks to try to drive or push a rubber disk into the other team's goal.

hol·i·day (häl'ə dā) **n.** a day on which most people do not have to work, often one set aside by law [Thanksgiving is a *holiday* in all States.]

hon·est (än'əst) **adj. 1** capable of being trusted; not stealing, cheating, or lying [an *honest* person].

hon·ey (hun'ē) **n. 1** a thick, sweet, yellow syrup that bees make from the nectar of flowers and store in honeycombs. **2** sweet one; darling: used in talking to someone dear to one [How are you, *honey*?]

hon·or (än'ər) **n. 1** great respect given because of worth, noble deeds, high rank, etc. [to pay *honor* to the geniuses of science]. **2** something done or given as a sign of respect [Madame Curie received many *honors* for her work.] **3** good name or reputation [You must uphold the *honor* of the family.] **4** a being true to what is right, honest, etc. [Her sense of *honor* kept her from cheating.] ◆**v.** to have or show great respect for [America *honors* the memory of Lincoln. *Honor* your father and your mother.] ◆**adj.** of or showing honor [an *honor* roll].

hope (hōp) *n.* a feeling that what one wants will happen [We gave up *hope* of being rescued.] ◆*v.* **1** to have hope; want and expect [I *hope* to see you soon.] **2** to want to believe [I *hope* I didn't overlook anybody.] —**hoped, hop'ing**

hour (our) *n.* **1** any of the 24 equal parts of a day; 60 minutes. **2** a particular time [At what *hour* shall we meet?]

how's (houz) **1** how is. **2** how has. **3** how does.

huge (hyōōj) *adj.* very large; immense [the *huge* trunk of the redwood tree]. —**huge'ly** *adv.* —**huge'ness** *n.*

hu·man (hyōō'mən) *adj.* that is a person or that has to do with people in general [a *human* being; *human* affairs]. ◆*n.* a person: *some people still prefer the full phrase* **human being**.

hum·ble (hum'bəl) *adj.* knowing one's own weaknesses and faults; not proud or bold; modest or meek [He became *humble* and asked her to forgive him.] —**hum'bler, hum'blest**

hun·gry (hun grē) *adj.* **1** wanting or needing food [Cold weather makes me *hungry*.] **2** having a strong desire; eager [*hungry* for praise]. —**hun'gri·er, hun'gri·est** —**hun'gri·ly** *adv.* —**hun'gri·ness** *n.*

hunt·er (hunt'ər) *n.* a person who hunts.

hur·ried (hur'ēd) *adj.* done or acting in a hurry; hasty [We ate a *hurried* lunch.] —**hur'ried·ly** *adv.*

hurt (hurt) *v.* **1** to cause pain or injury to; wound [The fall *hurt* my leg.] **2** to have pain [My head *hurts*.] **3** to harm or damage in some way [Water won't *hurt* this table top.] —**hurt, hurt'ing** ◆*n.* pain, injury, or harm [Warm water will ease the *hurt*.]

ice (īs) *n.* water frozen solid by cold [Water turns to *ice* at 0°C.] ◆*v.* **1** to change into ice; freeze [The lake *iced* over.] **2** to cover with icing, or frosting [to *ice* a cake]. —**iced, ic'ing**

i·cy (ī'sē) *adj.* **1** full of or covered with ice [*icy* streets]. **2** like ice; slippery or very cold [*icy* fingers]. —**i'ci·er, i'ci·est** —**i'ci·ly** *adv.* —**i'ci·ness** *n.*

I'd (īd) **1** I had. **2** I would. **3** I should.

I'll (īl) **1** I shall. **2** I will.

inch (inch) *n.* a unit for measuring length, equal to 1/12 foot. One inch equals 2.54 centimeters. —*pl.* **inch'es** ◆*v.* to move a little at a time [Lou *inched* along the narrow ledge.]

in·side (in'sīd') *n.* the side or part that is within; interior [Wash the windows on the *inside*.] ◆*adj.* on or in the inside; internal; indoor [*inside* work; an *inside* page].

in·stead (in sted') *adv.* in place of the other; as a substitute [If you have no cream, use milk *instead*.]

in·to (in'tōō *or* in'tə) *prep.* **1** to the inside of [to go *into* the house]. **2** to the form, condition, etc., of [The farm has been turned *into* a park. They got *into* trouble.]

is·n't (iz'ənt) is not.

itch (ich) *v.* to have a tickling feeling on the skin that makes one want to scratch; also, to cause to have this feeling [The wool shirt *itches* my skin.] ◆*n.* an itching feeling on the skin.

its (its) *pron.* of it or done by it: *the possessive form of* **it,** *thought of as an adjective* [Give the cat *its* dinner. The frost had done *its* damage.]

I've (īv) I have.

a	ask, fat
ā	ape, date
ä	car, lot
e	elf, ten
ē	even, meet
i	is, hit
ī	ice, fire
ō	open, go
ô	law, horn
oi	oil, point
ŏŏ	look, pull
ōō	ooze, tool
ou	out, crowd
u	up, cut
ʉ	fur, fern
ə	a in ago
	e in agent
	e in father
	i in unity
	o in collect
	u in focus
ch	chin, arch
ŋ	ring, singer
sh	she, dash
th	thin, truth
th	then, father
zh	s in pleasure

knight

jog (jäg) *v.* to move along slowly or steadily, but with a jolting motion. —**jogged, jog′ging** ◆*n.* a jogging pace; trot. —**jog′ger** *n.*

join (join) *v.* **1** to bring together; connect; fasten [We *joined* hands and stood in a circle.] **2** to become a part or member of [Paula has *joined* our club.] **3** to take part along with others [*Join* in the game.]

joke (jōk) *n.* anything said or done to get a laugh, as a funny story. ◆*v.* to tell or play jokes. —**joked, jok′ing** —**jok′ing·ly adv.**

keep (kēp) *v.* **1** to have or hold and not let go [He was *kept* after school. She kept her trim figure. Can you *keep* a secret?] **2** to hold for a later time; save [I *kept* the cake to eat later.] **3** to take care of; look after [He *keeps* house for himself.] **4** to stay or make stay as it is; last; continue [The fish will *keep* a while if you pack it in ice. *Keep* your engine running. *Keep* on walking.] —**kept, keep′ing**

kept ·(kept) *past tense and past participle of* **keep.**

kill (kil) *v.* **1** to cause the death of; make die; slay. **2** to put an end to; destroy or ruin [Her defeat *killed* all our hopes.] **3** to make time pass in doing unimportant things [an hour to *kill* before my train leaves]. ◆*n.* **1** the act of killing [to be in at the *kill*]. **2** an animal or animals killed [the lion's *kill*]. —**kill′er** *n.*

kind¹ (kīnd) *n.* sort or variety [all *kinds* of books].

kind² (kīnd) *adj.* **1** always ready to help others and do good; friendly, gentle, generous, sympathetic, etc. **2** showing goodness, generosity, sympathy, etc. [*kind* deeds; *kind* regards].

knee (nē) *n.* the joint between the thigh and the lower leg.

knew (nōō *or* nyōō) *past tense of* **know.**

knife (nīf) *n.* a tool having a flat, sharp blade set in a handle, used for cutting. —*pl.* **knives** ◆*v.* to cut or stab with a knife. —**knifed, knif′ing**

knight (nīt) *n.* a man in the Middle Ages who was given a military rank of honor after serving as a page and squire. Knights were supposed to be gallant and brave. ◆*v.* to give the rank of knight to.

knit (nit) *v.* **1** to make by looping yarn or thread together with special needles [to *knit* a scarf]. —**knit′ted** or **knit, knit′ting**

knives (nīvz) *n.* *plural of* **knife.**

knock (näk) *v.* **1** to hit as with the fist; especially, to rap on a door [Who is *knocking*?] **2** to hit and cause to fall [The dog *knocked* down the papergirl.] ◆*n.* a hard, loud blow, as with the fist; rap, as on a door.

knot (nät) *n.* **1** a lump, as in a string or ribbon, formed by a loop or a tangle drawn tight. **2** a fastening made by tying together parts or pieces of string, rope, etc. [Sailors make a variety of *knots.*] ◆*v.* **1** to tie or fasten with a knot; make a knot in. **2** to become tangled. —**knot′ted, knot′ting**

know (nō) *v.* **1** to be sure of or have the facts about [Do you *know* why grass is green? She *knows* the law.] **2** to have in one's mind or memory [The actress *knows* her lines.] **3** to be acquainted with [I *know* your brother well.] —**knew, known, know′ing**

lack (lak) *n.* **1** the condition of not having enough; shortage [*Lack* of money forced him to return home.] **2** the thing that is needed [Our most serious *lack* was fresh water.] ◆*v.* to be without or not have enough; need [The soil *lacks* nitrogen.]

la·dy (lā′dē) *n.* a woman, especially one who is polite and refined and has a sense of honor. —*pl.* **la′dies** ◆*adj.* that is a woman; female [a *lady* barber].

large (lärj) *adj.* of great size or amount; big [a *large* house; a *large* sum of money]. —**larg′er, larg′est** ◆*adv.* in a large way [Don't write so *large*.] —**large′ness** *n.*

late·ly (lāt′lē) *adv.* just before this time; not long ago; recently.

laugh (laf) *v.* to make a series of quick sounds with the voice that show one is amused or happy or, sometimes, that show scorn. One usually smiles or grins when laughing. ◆*n.* the act or sound of laughing.

law (lô) *n.* all the rules that tell people what they must or must not do, made by the government of a city, state, nation, etc. [the *law* of the land].

lawn (lôn) *n.* ground covered with grass that is cut short, as around a house.

leaf (lēf) *n.* **1** any of the flat, green parts growing from the stem of a plant or tree. **2** a sheet of paper in a book [Each side of a *leaf* is a page.] —*pl.* **leaves** —**leaf′less** *adj.*

learn (lɬrn) *v.* **1** to get some knowledge or skill, as by studying or being taught [I have *learned* to knit. Some people never *learn* from experience.] **2** to find out about something; come to know [When did you *learn* of his illness?] **3** to fix in the mind; memorize [*Learn* this poem by tomorrow.] —**learned** (lɬrnd) or **learnt** (lɬrnt), **learn′ing**

least (lēst) *adj.* smallest in size, amount, or importance [I haven't the *least* interest in the matter.] ◆*adv.* in the smallest amount or degree [I was *least* impressed by the music.] ◆*n.* the smallest in amount, degree, etc. [The *least* you can do is apologize. I'm not in the *least* interested.]

leave (lēv) *v.* to go away or go from [Rosa *left* early. Jose *leaves* the house at 8:00.] —**left, leav′ing**

leaves (lēvz) *n. plural of* **leaf**.

left¹ (left) *adj.* on or to the side that is toward the west when one faces north [the *left* hand; a *left* turn]. ◆*n.* the left side [Forks are placed at the *left* of the plate.] ◆*adv.* on or toward the left hand or side [Turn *left* here.]

left² (left) *past tense and past participle of* **leave**.

lev·el (lev′əl) *adj.* with no part higher than any other part; flat and even [a *level* plain]. ◆*n.* a small tube of liquid in a frame that is placed on a surface to see if the surface is level. A bubble in the liquid moves to the center of the tube when the frame is level. ◆*v.* to make level or flat [to *level* ground with a bulldozer]. —**lev′eled** or **lev′elled, lev′el·ing** or **lev′el·ling**

lie¹ (lī) *v.* **1** to stretch one's body in a flat position along the ground, a bed, etc. **2** to be in a flat position; rest [A book is *lying* on the table.] —**lay, lain, ly′ing**

lie² (lī) *n.* something said that is not true, especially if it is said on purpose to fool or trick someone. ◆*v.* to tell a lie; say what is not true. —**lied, ly′ing**

a	ask, fat
ā	ape, date
ä	car, lot
e	elf, ten
ē	even, meet
i	is, hit
ī	ice, fire
ō	open, go
ô	law, horn
oi	oil, point
͡oo	look, pull
͞oo	ooze, tool
ou	out, crowd
u	up, cut
ɬ	fur, fern
ə	a in ago
	e in agent
	e in father
	i in unity
	o in collect
	u in focus
ch	chin, arch
ŋ	ring, singer
sh	she, dash
th	thin, truth
th	then, father
zh	s in pleasure

life (līf) **n.** **1** the quality of plants and animals that makes it possible for them to take in food, grow, produce others of their kind, etc., and that makes them different from rocks, water, etc. [Death is the loss of *life*.] **2** a living thing; especially, a human being [The crash took six *lives*.] **3** the time that a person or thing is alive or lasts [Her *life* has just begun. What is the *life* of a battery?] —*pl.* **lives**

light[1] (līt) **n.** **1** brightness or radiance [the *light* of a candle; the *light* of love in his eyes]. **2** something that gives light, as a lamp [Turn off the *light*.] **3** a flame or spark to start something burning [a *light* for a pipe]. ◆ *adj.* **1** having light; not dark [It's getting *light* outside.] **2** having a pale color; fair [*light* hair]. ◆ *adv.* not brightly; in a pale way [a *light* green dress]. ◆ *v.* to set on fire or catch fire; burn [to *light* a match; the candle *lighted* at once].
—**light'ed** or **lit, light'ing**
—**light'ness n.**

light[2] (līt) **adj.** having little weight, especially for its size; not heavy [a *light* cargo; a *light* suit].

line (līn) **n.** **1** a cord, rope, string, etc. [a fishing *line*; a clothes*line*]. **2** a long, thin mark [*lines* made by a pen or pencil; *lines* formed in the face by wrinkles]. **3** a row of persons or things [a *line* of people waiting to get in; a *line* of words across a page]. ◆ *v.* to form a line along [Elms *line* the streets.] —**lined, lin'ing**

lit·tle (lit'l) **adj.** small in size; not large or big [a *little* house].
—**lit'tler** or **less** or **less'er, lit'tlest** or **least** ◆ *adv.* to a small degree; not very much [She is a *little* better.] —**less, least** ◆ **n.** a small amount [Have a *little* of this cake.] —**lit'tle·ness n.**

live[1] (liv) **v.** **1** to have life; be alive [No one *lives* forever.] **2** to make one's home; reside [We *live* on a farm.] —**lived, liv'ing**

live[2] (līv) **adj.** **1** having life; not dead. **2** that is broadcast while it is taking place; not photographed or recorded [a *live* television or radio program].

liv·ing (liv'iŋ) **adj.** having life; alive; not dead. ◆ **n.** **1** the fact of being alive. **2** the means of supporting oneself or one's family [He makes a *living* selling shoes.]

load (lōd) **n.** something that is carried or to be carried at one time [a heavy *load* on his back]. ◆ *v.* to put something to be carried into or upon a carrier [to *load* a bus with passengers; to *load* groceries into a cart].
—**load'er n.**

loaf (lōf) **n.** **1.** a portion of bread baked in one piece, usually oblong in shape. **2.** any food baked in this shape [a meat *loaf*].
—*pl.* **loaves**

long[1] (lôŋ) **adj.** **1** measuring much from end to end or from beginning to end; not short [a *long* board; a *long* trip; a *long* wait]. **2** taking a longer time to say than other sounds [The "a" in "cave" and the "i" in "hide" are *long*.] ◆ *adv.* for a long time [Don't be gone *long*.]

long[2] (lôŋ) **v.** to want very much; feel a strong desire for [We *long* to go home.]

loose (loos) **adj.** **1** not tied or held back; free [a *loose* end of wire]. **2** not tight or firmly fastened on or in something [*loose* clothing; a *loose* table leg]. ◆ *adv.* in a loose way [My coat hangs *loose*.] —**loose'ly adv.**
—**loose'ness n.**

lose (looz) **v.** **1** to put, leave, or drop, so as to be unable to find; misplace; mislay [He *lost* his keys somewhere.] **2** to fail to win; be defeated [We *lost* the football game.] —**lost, los'ing**

lost (lôst) *past tense and past participle of* **lose.** ◆ *adj.* that is mislaid, missing, destroyed, defeated, wasted, etc. [a *lost* hat; a *lost* child; a *lost* ship; a *lost* cause; *lost* time].

loud (loud) *adj.* **1** strong in sound; not soft or quiet [a *loud* noise; a *loud* bell]. **2** noisy [a *loud* party]. ◆*adv.* in a loud way. —**loud′ly** *adv.* —**loud′ness** *n.*

love·ly (luv′lē) *adj.* **1** very pleasing in looks or character; beautiful [a *lovely* person]. **2** very enjoyable: *used only in everyday talk* [We had a *lovely* time.] —**love′li·er, love′li·est** —**love′li·ness** *n.*

loy·al (loi′əl) *adj.* **1** faithful to one's country [a *loyal* citizen]. **2** faithful to one's family, duty, beliefs, etc. [a *loyal* friend; a *loyal* member]. —**loy′al·ly** *adv.*

Mm

mad (mad) *adj.* **1** angry [Don't be *mad* at us for leaving.] **2** crazy; insane. —**mad′der, mad′dest**

made (mād) *past tense and past participle of* **make.** ◆*adj.* built; put together; formed [a well-*made* house].

mag·ic (maj′ik) *n.* **1** the use of charms, spells, and rituals that are supposed to make things happen in an unnatural way [In fairy tales, *magic* is used to work miracles.] **2** the skill of doing puzzling tricks by moving the hands so fast as to fool those watching and by using boxes with false bottoms, hidden strings, etc.; sleight of hand. ◆*adj.* of or as if by magic.

maid (mād) *n.* **1** a maiden. **2** a girl or woman servant.

mail (māl) *n.* **1** letters, packages, etc., carried and delivered by a post office. **2** the system of picking up and delivering letters, papers, etc.; postal system [Send it by *mail*.] ◆*adj.* having to do with or carrying mail [a *mail* truck]. ◆*v.* ☆to send by mail; place in a mailbox. —**mail′a·ble** *adj.*

Maine (mān) a New England state of the U.S.: abbreviated **Me., ME**

make (māk) *v.* **1** to bring into being; build, create, produce, put together, etc. [to *make* a dress; to *make* a fire; to *make* plans; to *make* noise]. **2** to do, perform, carry on, etc. [to *make* a right turn; to *make* a speech]. —**made, mak′ing**

man (man) *n.* **1** an adult male human being. **2** any human being; person ["that all *men* are created equal"]. **3** the human race; mankind [*man's* conquest of space]. —*pl.* **men**

mark (märk) *n.* **1** a spot, stain, scratch, dent, etc., made on a surface. **2** a printed or written sign or label [punctuation *marks*; a trade*mark*]. **3** a grade or rating [a *mark* of B in spelling]. ◆*v.* **1** to make a mark or marks on. **2** to draw or write [*Mark* your name on your gym shoes.] **3** to give a grade to [to *mark* test papers].

mar·ry (mer′ē) *v.* **1** to join a man and a woman as husband and wife [A ship's captain may *marry* people at sea.] **2** to take as one's husband or wife [John Alden *married* Priscilla.] —**mar′ried, mar′ry·ing**

may (mā) *a helping verb used with other verbs and meaning:* **1** to be possible or likely [It *may* rain.] **2** to be allowed or have permission [You *may* go.] **3** to be able to as a result [Be quiet so that we *may* hear.] *May* is also used in exclamations to mean "I or we hope or wish" [*May* you win!] —The past tense is **might.**

may·be (mā′bē) *adv.* it may be; perhaps.

a	ask, fat
ā	ape, date
ä	car, lot
e	elf, ten
ē	even, meet
i	is, hit
ī	ice, fire
ō	open, go
ô	law, horn
oi	oil, point
ōo	look, pull
ōō	ooze, tool
ou	out, crowd
u	up, cut
u	fur, fern
ə	a in ago
	e in agent
	e in father
	i in unity
	o in collect
	u in focus
ch	chin, arch
ŋ	ring, singer
sh	she, dash
th	thin, truth
th	then, father
zh	s in pleasure

money

mouse

mel·o·dy (mel′ə dē) *n.* **1** an arrangement of musical tones in a series so as to form a tune; often, the main tune in the harmony of a musical piece [The *melody* is played by the oboes.] **2** any pleasing series of sounds [a *melody* sung by birds]. —*pl.* **mel′o·dies**

melt (melt) *v.* **1** to change from a solid to a liquid, as by heat [The bacon fat *melted* in the frying pan.] **2** to dissolve [The candy *melted* in my mouth.]

men (men) *n. plural of* **man.**

mice (mīs) *n. plural of* **mouse.**

might[1] (mīt) *past tense of* **may.**

might[2] (mīt) *n.* great strength, force, or power [Pull with all your *might*.]

mile (mīl) *n.* a standard measure of length, equal to 5,280 feet or 1,760 yards or 1.6093 kilometers.

mix (miks) *v.* to put, stir, or come together to form a single, blended thing [*Mix* red and yellow paint to get orange.] — **mixed** or **mixt** (mikst), **mix′ing** ◆ *n.* a mixture. —*pl.* **mix′es**

Monday (mun′dā) *n.* the second day of the week.

mon·ey (mun′ē) *n.* coins of gold, silver, or other metal, or paper bills to take the place of these, issued by a government for use in buying and selling. —*pl.* **mon′eys** or **mon′ies**

mood (mood) *n.* the way one feels; frame of mind [She's in a happy *mood* today.]

moon·light (moon′līt) *n.* the light of the moon.

morn·ing (môrn′iŋ) *n.* the early part of the day, from midnight to noon or, especially, from dawn to noon.

most·ly (mōst′lē) *adv.* mainly; chiefly.

☆**mo·tel** (mō tel′) *n.* a hotel for those traveling by car, usually with a parking area easily reached from each room.

moth (môth *or* mäth) *n.* an insect similar to the butterfly, but usually smaller and less brightly colored and flying mostly at night —*pl.* **moths** (mothz *or* mäths)

mouse (mous) *n.* **1** a small, gnawing animal found in houses and fields throughout the world. **2** a timid person. ☆**3** a small device moved by hand, as on a flat surface, so as to make the cursor move on a computer terminal screen. —*pl.* **mice** (mīs)

muf·fler (muf′lər) *n.* **1** a scarf worn around the throat for warmth. **2** a thing used to deaden noise, as ☆a part fastened to the exhaust pipe of an automobile engine.

mul·ti·ply (mul′tə plī) *v.* **1** to become more, greater, etc.; increase [Our troubles *multiplied*.] **2** to repeat a certain figure a certain number of times [If you *multiply* 10 by 4, or repeat 10 four times, you get the product 40.] —**mul′ti·plied, mul′ti·ply·ing**

mu·sic (myōō′zik) *n.* **1** the art of putting tones together in various melodies, rhythms, and harmonies to form compositions for singing or playing on instruments [She teaches *music*.] **2** any series of pleasing sounds [the *music* of birds].

must·n't (mus′ənt) must not.

my·self (mī self′) *pron.* **1** my own self. *This form of* **I** *is used when the object is the same as the subject of the verb* [I hurt *myself*.] **2** my usual or true self [I'm not *myself* today.] *Myself is also used to give force to the subject* [I'll do it *myself*.]

nee·dle (nēd′əl) **n.** **1** a small, slender piece of steel with a sharp point and a hole for thread, used for sewing. **2** a short, slender piece of metal, often tipped with diamond, that moves in the grooves of a phonograph record to pick up the vibrations. **3** the thin, pointed leaf of a pine, spruce, etc. **4** the sharp, very slender metal tube at the end of a hypodermic syringe.

New York (yôrk) **1** a state in the northeastern part of the U.S.: abbreviated **N.Y.**, **NY** **2** a seaport in southeastern New York State, on the Atlantic Ocean; the largest city in the U.S.: *often called* **New York City.**

next (nekst) **adj.** coming just before or just after; nearest or closest [the *next* person in line; the *next* room; *next* Monday]. ◆*adv.* **1** in the nearest place, time, etc. [She sits *next* to me in school. Please wait on me *next*.] **2** at the first chance after this [What should I do *next*?]

nice (nīs) **adj.** good, pleasant, agreeable, pretty, kind, polite, etc.: *used as a general word showing that one likes something* [a *nice* time; a *nice* dress; a *nice* neighbor]. —**nic′er, nic′est** —**nice′ly adv.**

night (nīt) **n.** the time of darkness between sunset and sunrise. ◆*adj.* of, for, or at night [*night* school].

nine (nīn) **n., adj.** one more than eight; the number 9.

ninth (nīnth) **adj.** coming after eight others; 9th in order. ◆*n.* one of nine equal parts of something; 1/9.

noise (noiz) **n.** sound, especially a loud, harsh, or confused sound [the *noise* of fireworks; *noises* of a city street]. ◆*v.* to make public by telling; spread [to *noise* a rumor about]. —**noised, nois′ing**

nois·y (noi′zē) **adj.** **1** making noise [a *noisy* bell]. **2** full of noise [a *noisy* theater]. —**nois′i·er, nois′i·est** —**nois′i·ly adv.** —**nois′i·ness n.**

note (nōt) **n.** **1** a word, phrase, or sentence written down to help one remember something one has heard, read, thought, etc. [The students kept *notes* on the lecture.] **2** a short letter. **3** close attention; notice [Take *note* of what I say.] **4** a musical tone; also, the symbol for such a tone, showing how long it is to be sounded. Where it is placed on the staff tells how high or low it is.

noun (noun) **n.** a word that is the name of a person, thing, action, quality, etc. A phrase or a clause can be used in a sentence as a noun ["Boy," "water," and "truth" are *nouns*.]

No·vem·ber (nō vem′bər) **n.** the eleventh month of the year, which has 30 days: abbreviated **Nov.**

nurse (nurs) **n.** a person who has been trained to take care of sick people, help doctors, etc. ◆*v.* to take care of sick people, as a nurse does. —**nursed, nurs′ing**

ob·ject (äb′jekt) **n.** **1** a thing that can be seen or touched; something that takes up space [That brown *object* is a purse.] **2** a person or thing toward which one turns one's thoughts, feelings, or actions [the *object* of my affection].

needle

a	ask, fat
ā	ape, date
ä	car, lot
e	elf, ten
ē	even, meet
i	is, hit
ī	ice, fire
ō	open, go
ô	law, horn
oi	oil, point
o͝o	look, pull
o͞o	ooze, tool
ou	out, crowd
u	up, cut
ʉ	fur, fern
ə	a in ago
	e in agent
	e in father
	i in unity
	o in collect
	u in focus
ch	chin, arch
ŋ	ring, singer
sh	she, dash
th	thin, truth
th	then, father
zh	s in pleasure

Oc·to·ber (äk tō′bər) *n.* the tenth month of the year, which has 31 days: abbreviated **Oct.**

O·hi·o (ō hī′ō) **1** a state in the north central part of the U.S.: abbreviated **O., OH 2** a river that flows along the southern borders of Ohio, Indiana, and Illinois to the Mississippi. —**O·hi′o·an** *adj., n.*

oint·ment (ɔint′mənt) *n.* an oily cream rubbed on the skin to heal it or make it soft and smooth; salve.

once (wuns) *adv.* **1** one time [We eat together *once* a week.] **2** at some time in the past; formerly [They were rich *once*.] ◆*conj.* as soon as; whenever [*Once* the horse tires, it will quit.] ◆*n.* one time [I'll go this *once*.]

on·ly (ōn′lē) *adj.* without any other or others of the same kind; sole [the *only* suit I own; their *only* friends]. ◆*adv.* and no other; and no more; just; merely [I have *only* fifty cents. Bite off *only* what you can chew.]

or·der (ôr′dər) *n.* **1** the way in which things are placed or follow one another; arrangement [The entries in this dictionary are in alphabetical *order*.] **2** a direction telling someone what to do, given by a person with authority; command [The general's *orders* were quickly obeyed.] **3** a request for something that one wants to buy or receive [Mail your *order* for flower seeds today.] ◆*v.* **1** to tell what to do; give an order to [The captain *ordered* the troops to charge.] **2** to ask for something one wants to buy or receive [Please *order* some art supplies for the class.]

our (ɔur) *pron.* of us or done by us. *This possessive form of* **we** *is used before a noun and thought of as an adjective* [*our* car; *our* work].

our·selves (our selvz′) *pron.* **1** our own selves. *This form of* **we** *is used when the object is the same as the subject of the verb* [We hurt *ourselves*.] **2** our usual or true selves [We are not *ourselves* today.] *Ourselves is also used to give force to the subject* [We built it *ourselves*.]

ox (äks) *n.* any animal of a group that chew their cud and have cloven hoofs, including the buffalo, bison, etc. —*pl.* **ox·en** (äks′ən)

ox·ford (äks′fərd) *n.* a low shoe that is laced over the instep: *also called* **oxford shoe.**

OX

oxford

Pp

pack (pak) *n.* a bundle of things that is tied or wrapped [a hiker's *pack*]. ◆*v.* **1** to tie or wrap together in a bundle [I *packed* books at the book sale.] **2** to put things together in a box, trunk, or suitcase for carrying or storing [to *pack* a suitcase.]

page¹ (pāj) *n.* one side of a leaf of paper in a book, newspaper, letter, etc. ◆*v.* to turn pages in looking quickly [to *page* through a book]. —**paged, pag′ing**

page² (pāj) *n.* a boy, or sometimes a girl, who runs errands and carries messages in a hotel, office building, or legislature. ◆*v.* ☆to try to find a person by calling out the name, as a hotel page does. —**paged, pag′ing**

pair (per) *n.* **1** two things of the same kind that are used together; set of two [a *pair* of skates]. **2** a single thing with two parts that are used together [a *pair* of eyeglasses; a *pair* of pants]. ◆*v.* to arrange in or form a pair or pairs; match.

pa·per (pā′pər) *n.* **1** a thin material in sheets, made from wood pulp, rags, etc., and used to write or print on, to wrap or decorate with, etc. **2** a single sheet of this material. **3** something written or printed on paper, as an essay, report, etc. [The teacher is grading a set of *papers*.]

pa·rade (pə rād′) *n.* any march or procession, as to celebrate a holiday [a Fourth of July *parade*]. ◆*v.* to march in a parade. —**pa·rad′ed, pa·rad′ing**

pare (per) *v.* to cut or trim away the rind or covering of something; peel [to *pare* a potato; to *pare* the bark from a tree]. —**pared, par′ing**

par·ty (pär′tē) *n.* **1** a gathering of people to have a good time [a birthday *party*]. **2** a group of people working or acting together [a hunting *party*]. —*pl.* **par′ties**

past (past) *adj.* gone by; ended; over [What is *past* is finished.] ◆*n.* the time that has gone by [That's all in the *past*.] ◆*prep.* later than or farther than; beyond [ten minutes *past* two; *past* the city limits].

patch (pach) *n.* **1** a piece of cloth, metal, etc., put on to mend a hole, tear, or worn spot. **2** a bandage put on a wound or a pad worn over an injured eye. **3** an area or spot [*patches* of blue sky]. ◆*v.* to put a patch or patches on [to *patch* the worn elbows of a coat].

pear (per) *n.* a soft, juicy fruit, often yellow or green, that is round at one end and narrows toward the stem.

peo·ple (pē′pəl) *n.* human beings; persons.

per·haps (pər haps′) *adv.* possibly; maybe [*Perhaps* it will rain. Did you, *perhaps*, lose it?]

pe·ri·od (pir′ē əd) *n.* **1** the time that goes by during which something goes on, a cycle is repeated, etc. [the medieval *period*; a *period* of hot weather]. **2** the mark of punctuation (.) used at the end of most sentences or often after abbreviations.

per·son (pur′sən) *n.* a human being; man, woman, or child [every *person* in this room].

☆**phone** (fōn) *n., v.* *a shorter word for* **telephone**: *used only in everyday talk.* —**phoned, phon′ing**

pick[1] (pik) *n.* a heavy metal tool with a pointed head, used for breaking up rock, soil, etc.

pick[2] (pik) *v.* **1** to choose or select [The judges *picked* the winner.] **2** to scratch or dig at with the fingers or with something pointed [to *pick* the teeth with a toothpick]. **3** to pluck or gather with the fingers or hands [to *pick* flowers]. ◆*n.* the act of choosing or the thing chosen; choice [Take your *pick* of these books.] —**pick′er** *n.*

pinch (pinch) *v.* to squeeze between a finger and the thumb or between two surfaces [He gently *pinched* the baby's cheek. She *pinched* her finger in the door.] ◆*n.* **1** a pinching; squeeze; nip [a *pinch* on the arm]. **2** the amount that can be picked up between the finger and thumb [a *pinch* of salt].

pi·rate (pī′rət) *n.* **1** a person who attacks and robs ships on the ocean. **2** a person who uses copyrighted or patented work without permission.

pitch (pich) *v.* **1** to throw or toss [*Pitch* the newspaper on the porch.] **2** to set up; make ready for use [to *pitch* a tent]. **3** to slope downward [The roof *pitches* sharply.] ◆*n.* **1** anything pitched or thrown [The wild *pitch* hit the batter.] **2** the highness or lowness of a musical sound.

pick

a	ask, fat
ā	ape, date
ä	car, lot
e	elf, ten
ē	even, meet
i	is, hit
ī	ice, fire
ō	open, go
ô	law, horn
oi	oil, point
‍oo	look, pull
‾oo	ooze, tool
ou	out, crowd
u	up, cut
ʉ	fur, fern
ə	a in ago
	e in agent
	e in father
	i in unity
	o in collect
	u in focus
ch	chin, arch
ŋ	ring, singer
sh	she, dash
th	thin, truth
th	then, father
zh	s in pleasure

place (plās) *n.* **1** a space taken up or used by a person or thing [Please take your *places*.] **2** a house, apartment, etc., where one lives [Visit me at my *place*.] **3** rank or position, especially in a series [I finished the race in fifth *place*.] ◆*v.* **1** to put in a certain place, position, etc. [*Place* the pencil on the desk.] **2** to finish in a certain position in a contest [Lynn *placed* sixth in the race.] —**placed, plac′ing**

plan (plan) *n.* **1** a method or way of doing something that has been thought out ahead of time [vacation *plans*]. **2** a drawing that shows how the parts of a building or piece of ground are arranged [floor *plans* of a house; a *plan* of the battlefield]. ◆*v.* **1** to think out a way of making or doing something [They *planned* their escape carefully.] **2** to make a drawing or diagram of beforehand [An architect is *planning* our new school.] **3** to have in mind; intend [I *plan* to visit Hawaii soon.] —**planned, plan′ning**

plane (plān) *n.* *a short form of* **airplane.**

plant (plant) *n.* **1** any living thing that cannot move about by itself, has no sense organs, and usually makes its own food by photosynthesis [Trees, shrubs, and vegetables are *plants*.] **2** the machinery, buildings, etc., of a factory or business. ◆*v.* to put into the ground so that it will grow [to *plant* corn].

play (plā) *v.* **1** to have fun; amuse oneself [children *playing* in the sand]. **2** to do in fun [to *play* a joke on a friend]. **3** to take part in a game or sport [to *play* golf]. **4** to perform music on [He *plays* the piano.] **5** to give out sounds: said of a phonograph, tape recorder, etc. ◆*n.* **1** something done just for fun or to amuse oneself;

recreation [She has little time for *play*.] **2** fun; joking [Jan said it in *play*.] **3** the playing of a game [Rain halted *play*.] **4** a story that is acted out, as on a stage, on radio or television, etc.; drama.

play·ful (plā′fəl) *adj.* **1** fond of play or fun; lively; frisky [a *playful* puppy]. **2** said or done in fun; joking [She gave her brother a *playful* shove.] —**play′ful·ly** *adv.* —**play′ful·ness** *n.*

please (plēz) *v.* **1** to give pleasure to; satisfy [Few things *please* me more than a good book.] **2** to be kind enough to: *used in asking for something politely* [*Please* pass the salt.] **3** to wish or desire; like [Do as you *please*.] —**pleased, pleas′ing**

plen·ty (plen′tē) *n.* a supply that is large enough; all that is needed [We have *plenty* of help.]

plumb·er (plum′ər) *n.* a person whose work is putting in and repairing the pipes and fixtures of water and gas systems in a building.

point (point) *n.* **1** a position or place; location [the *point* where the roads meet]. **2** a dot in printing or writing [a decimal *point*]. **3** a unit used in measuring or scoring [A touchdown is worth six *points*.] **4** a sharp end [the *point* of a needle]. **5** an important or main idea or fact [the *point* of a joke]. ◆*v.* to aim one's finger [He *pointed* to the book he wanted.]

pol·ish (päl′ish) *v.* to make smooth and bright or shiny, usually by rubbing [to *polish* a car with wax]. ◆*n.* **1** brightness or shine on a surface [a wood floor with a fine *polish*]. **2** a substance used for polishing [shoe *polish*]. —*pl.* **pol′ish·es**

po·lite (pə līt′) *adj.* having or showing good manners; thoughtful of others; courteous [a *polite* note of thanks]. —**po·lite′ly** *adv.* —**po·lite′ness** *n.*

pool[1] (po͞ol) *n.* **1** a small pond. **2** a puddle. **3** *a shorter form of* **swimming pool**.

pool[2] (po͞ol) *n.* a game of billiards played on a table, called a **pool table,** having six pockets into which the balls are knocked.

po·ta·to (pə tāt′ō) *n.* a plant whose tuber, or thick, starchy underground stem, is used as a vegetable. —*pl.* **po·ta′toes**

pound[1] (pound) *n.* a unit of weight, equal to 16 ounces in avoirdupois weight or 12 ounces in troy weight.   One pound avoirdupois equals 453.59 grams.

pound[2] (pound) *v.* **1** to hit with many heavy blows; hit hard [to *pound* on a door]. **2** to beat in a heavy way; throb [Her heart *pounded* from the exercise.] ◆*n.* a hard blow or the sound of it.

pound[3] (pound) *n.* a closed-in place for keeping animals, especially stray ones [a dog *pound*].

pow·er (pou′ər) *n.* **1** ability to do or act [Lobsters have the *power* to grow new claws.] **2** strength or force [the *power* of a boxer's blows]. **3** force or energy that can be put to work [electric *power*]. **4** the ability to control others; authority [the *power* of the law]. ◆*adj.* worked by electricity or other kind of power [a *power* saw].

pray (prā) *v.* **1** to talk or recite a set of words to God in worship or in asking for something. **2** to beg or ask for seriously ["*Pray* tell me" means "I beg you to tell me."]

pret·ty (prit′ē) *adj.* pleasant to look at or hear, especially in a delicate, dainty, or graceful way [a *pretty* girl; a *pretty* voice; a *pretty* garden]. —**pret′ti·er, pret′ti·est** ◆*adv.* somewhat; rather [I'm *pretty* tired.] ◆*v.* to make pretty [She *prettied* up her room.] —**pret′tied, pret′ty·ing** —**pret′ti·ly** *adv.*   —**pret′ti·ness** *n.*

prize (prīz) *n.* **1** something offered or given to a winner of a contest, lottery, etc. [The first *prize* is a bicycle.] **2** anything worth trying to get [Her friendship would be a great *prize*.]

prom·ise (präm′is) *n.* an agreement to do or not to do something; vow [to make and keep a *promise*]. ◆*v.* to make a promise to [I *promised* them I'd arrive at ten.] —**prom′ised, prom′is·ing**

proud (proud) *adj.* **1** having proper respect for oneself, one's work, one's family, etc. [He is too *proud* to ask for help.] **2** thinking too highly of oneself; conceited; vain or haughty [They are too *proud* to say hello to us.] **3** feeling or causing pride or pleasure [his *proud* mother; a *proud* moment]. —**proud′ly** *adv.*

pud·dle (pud′əl) *n.* a small pool of water or water mixed with earth [*puddles* after the rain; a mud *puddle*].

pup·py (pup′ē) *n.* a young dog. —*pl.* **pup′pies**

push (poosh) *v.* **1** to press against so as to move; shove [to *push* a stalled car; to *push* a stake into the ground]. **2** to urge the use, sale, etc., of [The company is *pushing* its new product.] ◆*n.* the act of pushing; a shove or thrust [One hard *push* opened the door.]

potato

Qq

quite (kwīt) *adv.* **1** completely; entirely [I haven't *quite* finished eating.] **2** really; truly [You are *quite* a musician.] **3** very or somewhat [It's *quite* warm outside.]

a	ask, fat
ā	ape, date
ä	car, lot
e	elf, ten
ē	even, meet
i	is, hit
ī	ice, fire
ō	open, go
ô	law, horn
oi	oil, point
oo	look, pull
ōō	ooze, tool
ou	out, crowd
u	up, cut
ʉ	fur, fern
ə	a in ago
	e in agent
	e in father
	i in unity
	o in collect
	u in focus
ch	chin, arch
ŋ	ring, singer
sh	she, dash
th	thin, truth
th	then, father
zh	s in pleasure

rac·coon (ra kōōn′) *n.* a furry animal having a long tail with black rings and black face markings that look like a mask.

race (rās) *n.* a contest, as among runners, swimmers, cars, boats, etc., to see who can go fastest. ◆ *v.* **1** to take part in a race [How many planes are *racing*?] **2** to have a race with [I'll *race* you to the corner.] **3** to go very fast [Her eye *raced* over the page.] —**raced, rac′ing**

rain (rān) *n.* **1** water that falls to the earth in drops formed from the moisture in the air. **2** the falling of such drops; a shower [Sunshine followed the *rain*.] ◆ *v.* to fall as rain [It is *raining*.]

raise (rāz) *v.* **1** to cause to rise; lift [*Raise* your hand if you have a question. *Raise* the window.] **2** to make larger, greater, higher, louder, etc. [to *raise* prices; to *raise* one's voice]. **3** to bring up; take care of; support [to *raise* a family]. —**raised, rais′ing** ◆ *n.* a making or becoming larger; especially, an increase in salary or wages.

rash (rash) *n.* a breaking out of red spots on the skin [The measles gave her a *rash*.]

re- *a prefix meaning:* **1** again [To *reappear* is to appear again.] **2** back [To *repay* is to pay back.]

read¹ (rēd) *v.* **1** to get the meaning of something written or printed by understanding its letters, signs, or numbers [I *read* the book. She *read* the gas meter. Can you *read* music?] **2** to speak printed or written words aloud [*Read* the story to me.] —**read** (red), **read′ing**

read² (red) *past tense and past participle of* **read¹**. ◆ *adj.* having knowledge got from reading; informed [They are both well-*read*.]

read·y (red′ē) *adj.* prepared to act or to be used at once [Is everyone *ready* to leave? Your bath is *ready*.] —**read′i·er, read′i·est** ◆ *v.* to prepare [to *ready* the house for guests]. —**read′ied, read′y·ing** —**read′i·ness** *n.*

re·ap·ply (rē ə plī′) *v.* to put or spread on again [*Reapply* glue to that corner.] —**re·ap·plied, re·ap·ply′ing**

re·as·sign (rē ə sīn′) *v.* to give out as a task again [The teacher *reassigned* the same homework.]

re·build (rē bild′) *v.* to build again, especially something that was damaged, ruined, etc. —**re·built′, re·build′ing**

re·do (rē dōō) *v.* **1** to do again **2** to redecorate, as a room. —**re·did′, re·done′, re·do′ing**

re·fill (rē fil′) *v.* to fill again. ◆ *n.* (re′fil) **1** something to refill a special container [a *refill* for a ballpoint pen]. **2** any extra filling of a prescription for medicine. —**re·fill′a·ble** *adj.*

re·form (rē fôrm′) *v.* **1** to make better by getting rid of faults, wrongs, etc.; improve [to *reform* working conditions in a factory; to *reform* a criminal]. **2** to become better; give up one's bad ways [The outlaw *reformed* and became a better citizen.] ◆ *n.* correction of faults or evils, as in government.

re·fresh (rē fresh′) *v.* to make fresh again; bring back into good condition [A soft rain *refreshed* the wilted plants. She *refreshed* herself with a short nap. *Refresh* my memory by playing the piece again.]

re·lease (rē lēs′) *v.* to set free or relieve [*Release* the bird from the cage.] —**re·leased′, re·leas′ing**

re·mind (rē mīnd′) *v.* to make remember or think of [*Remind* me to pay the gas bill.]

re·name (rē nām′) **v.** to give a new or different name to [Ceylon was *renamed* Sri Lanka.] —**re·named′, re·nam′ing**

re·new (rē noo͞′ *or* rē nyoo͞′) **v.** **1** to make new or fresh again; restore [*Renew* that old table by painting it.] **2** to give or get again for a new period of time [It is time to *renew* your subscription.] —**re·new′al n.**

re·pay (rē pā′) **v.** **1** to pay back [to *repay* a loan]. **2** to do or give something to someone in return for some favor, service, etc., received [to *repay* a kindness]. —**re·paid′, re·pay′ing** —**re·pay′ment n.**

re·place (rē plās′) **v.** **1** to put back in the right place [*Replace* the tools on my bench when you are through.] **2** to take the place of [Many workers have been *replaced* by computers.] **3** to put another in the place of one used, lost, broken, etc. [to *replace* a worn tire]. —**re·placed′, re·plac′ing**

re·ply (rē plī′) **v.** to answer by saying or doing something [to *reply* to a question; to *reply* to the enemy's fire with a counter-attack]. —**re·plied′, re·ply′ing** ◆**n.** an answer. —*pl.* **re·plies′**

re·run (rē run′) **v.** to run again. —**re·ran′, re·run′ning** ◆**n.** (rē′run) ☆ a repeat showing of a movie, taped TV program, etc.

ret·i·na (ret′n ə) **n.** the part at the back of the eyeball, made up of special cells that react to light. The image picked up by the lens of the eye is formed on the retina.

re·triev·er (rē trēv′ər) **n.** a dog that is trained to retrieve game in hunting.

re·write (rē rīt′) **v.** to write again or in different words; revise [to *rewrite* a story]. —**re·wrote′, re·writ′ten, re·writ′ing**

rich (rich) **adj.** **1** having wealth; owning much money or property; wealthy. **2** having much of something; well supplied [Tomatoes are *rich* in vitamin C.] **3** full of fats, or fats and sugar [*rich* foods]. —**rich′ly adv.** —**rich′ness n.**

ring¹ (riŋ) **v.** **1** to cause a bell to sound [*Ring* the doorbell.] **2** to make the sound of a bell [The phone *rang*.] —**rang** or rarely **rung, rung, ring′ing** ◆**n.** **1** the sound of a bell. **2** a telephone call [Give me a *ring* soon.] —**ring′er n.**

ring² (riŋ) **n.** **1** a thin band of metal, plastic, etc., shaped like a circle and worn on the finger or used to hold or fasten things [a wedding *ring*; a curtain *ring*]. **2** a line or edge forming a circle [a *ring* around the moon]. **3** an enclosed space for contests, shows, etc. [the *ring* of a circus; a boxing *ring*]. ◆**v.** to make a circle around or form in a ring. —**ringed, ring′ing** —**ringed adj.** —**ring′er n.**

rise (rīz) **v.** **1** to stand up or get up from a lying or sitting position. **2** to become greater, higher, or stronger [The temperature *rose*. Prices are *rising*. Her voice *rose*.] —**rose, ris′en, ris′ing** ◆**n.** **1** a piece of ground higher than that around it [There's a good view of the countryside from the top of the *rise*.] **2** the fact of becoming greater, higher, etc.; increase [a *rise* in prices].

rock¹ (räk) **n.** a large mass of stone.

rock² (räk) **v.** to move or swing back and forth or from side to side [to *rock* a cradle]. ◆**n.** a rocking movement.

roof (roo͞f *or* roof) **n.** **1** the outside top covering of a building. **2** anything like a roof in the way it is placed or used [the *roof* of the mouth; the *roof* of a car]. —**roof′less adj.**

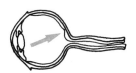

retina

a	ask, fat
ā	ape, date
ä	car, lot
e	elf, ten
ē	even, meet
i	is, hit
ī	ice, fire
ō	open, go
ô	law, horn
oi	oil, point
oo	look, pull
oo	ooze, tool
ou	out, crowd
u	up, cut
u	fur, fern
ə	a in ago
	e in agent
	e in father
	i in unity
	o in collect
	u in focus
ch	chin, arch
ŋ	ring, singer
sh	she, dash
th	thin, truth
th	then, father
zh	s in pleasure

rough (ruf) *adj.* **1** not smooth or level; uneven [a *rough* road; *rough* fur]. **2** full of noise and wild action; disorderly [*rough* play]. **3** not gentle or mild, as in manners; rude, harsh, etc. [*rough* language]. **4** having little comfort or luxury [the *rough* life of a pioneer].

round (round) *adj.* shaped like a ball, a circle, or a tube; having an outline that forms a circle or curve [The world is *round*. Wheels are *round*. The ship has a *round* smokestack.] ◆*n.* a short song for two or more persons or groups, in which the second starts when the first gets to the second phrase, and so on.

ru·ler (rōōl'ər) *n.* a straight, thin strip of wood, metal, or plastic used in drawing straight lines and measuring.

rush (rush) *v.* **1** to move, send, take, etc., with great speed [I *rushed* from the room. We *rushed* him to a hospital.] **2** to act in haste, without thinking carefully [Don't *rush* into marriage.] ◆*adj.* that must be done or sent in a hurry [a *rush* order].

sail

Ss

said (sed) *past tense and past participle of* **say.** ◆*adj.* named or mentioned before [The *said* contract is no longer in force.]

sail (sāl) *n.* **1** a sheet of heavy cloth such as canvas, used on a ship or boat to move it by catching the wind. **2** a trip in a ship or boat, especially one moved by sails [Let's go for a *sail*.] ◆*v.* **1** to travel on water [This liner *sails* between Miami and New York.] **2** to move smoothly [a hawk *sailing* in the sky].

sale (sāl) *n.* **1** the act of selling, or exchanging something for money [The clerk made ten *sales* today.] **2** a special selling of goods at prices lower than usual [a clearance *sale*].

sam·ple (sam'pəl) *n.* a part or piece that shows what the whole group or thing is like; specimen or example [little pieces of wallpaper for *samples*; a *sample* of his typing]. ◆*adj.* that is a sample [a *sample* page of the book]. ◆*v.* to test by trying a sample [He *sampled* the basket of grapes.] —**sam'pled, sam'pling**

sat·is·fy (sat'is fī') *v.* to meet the needs or wishes of; to content; to please [Only first prize will *satisfy* him.] —**sat'is·fied', sat'is·fy'ing**

Sat·ur·day (sat'ər dē) *n.* the seventh and last day of the week.

sau·sage (sô'sij *or* sä'sij) *n.* pork or other meat, chopped up and seasoned and, usually, stuffed into a tube made of thin skin.

save (sāv) *v.* **1** to rescue or keep from harm or danger [He was *saved* from drowning.] **2** to keep or store up for future use [She *saved* her money for a vacation.] —**saved, sav'ing** —**sav'er** *n.*

scale¹ (skāl) *n.* **1** a series of marks along a line, with regular spaces in-between, used for measuring [A Celsius thermometer has a basic *scale* of 100 degrees.] **2** the way that the size of a map, model, or drawing compares with the size of the thing that it stands for [One inch on a map of this *scale* equals 100 miles of real distance.] **3** a series of musical tones arranged in order from the highest to the lowest or from the lowest to the highest. —**on a large scale,** to a large extent.

scale² (skāl) *n.* any of the thin, flat, hard plates that cover and protect certain fish and reptiles.

scale³ (skāl) *n.* **1** either of the shallow pans of a balance. **2** *often* **scales,** *pl.* the balance itself; also, any device or machine for weighing.

scarf (skärf) *n.* a long or broad piece of cloth worn about the head, neck, or shoulders for warmth or decoration. —*pl.* **scarves** (skärvz) or **scarfs**

scent (sent) *n.* **1** a smell; odor [the *scent* of apple blossoms]. **2** the sense of smell [Lions hunt partly by *scent.*]

school¹ (skool) *n.* **1** a place, usually a special building, for teaching and learning, as a public school, dancing school, college, etc. **2** the students and teachers of a school [an assembly for the *school*]. ◆*adj.* of or for a school or schools [our *school* band].

school² (skool) *n.* a large group of fish or water animals of the same kind swimming together [a *school* of porpoises]. ◆*v.* to swim together in a school.

scold (skōld) *v.* to find fault with someone in an angry way [I *scolded* her for being late.]

scoop (skoop) *n.* **1** a kitchen tool like a small shovel, used to take up sugar, flour, etc., or one with a small, round bowl for dishing up ice cream, etc. **2** the amount taken up at one time by a scoop [three *scoops* of ice cream]. ◆*v.* to take up as with a scoop [We *scooped* it up with our hands.]

scram·ble (skram′bəl) *v.* to cook eggs while stirring the mixed whites and yolks. —**scram′bled, scram′bling**

scratch (skrach) *v.* **1** to mark or cut the surface of slightly with something sharp [Thorns *scratched* her legs. Our cat *scratched* the chair with its claws.] **2** to rub or scrape, as with the nails, to relieve itching [to *scratch* a mosquito bite]. **3** to cross out by drawing lines through [She *scratched* out what he had written.] ◆*n.* **1** a mark or cut made in a surface by something sharp. **2** a slight wound. **3** a harsh, grating sound [the *scratch* of chalk on a blackboard].

scream (skrēm) *v.* to give a loud, shrill cry, as in fright or pain [They *screamed* as the roller coaster hurtled downward.] ◆*n.* a loud, shrill cry or sound; shriek.

screen (skrēn) *n.* **1** a mesh woven loosely of wires so as to leave small openings between them. Screens are used in windows, doors, etc., to keep insects out. **2** a covered frame or curtain used to hide, separate, or protect. **3** a surface on which movies, television pictures, etc., are shown.

seat (sēt) *n.* **1** a thing to sit on, as a chair, bench, etc. **2** a place to sit or the right to sit [to buy two *seats* for the opera; to win a *seat* in the Senate]. ◆*v.* **1** to cause to sit; put in or on a seat [*Seat* yourself quickly.] **2** to have seats for [This car *seats* six people.]

see (sē) *v.* **1** to be aware of through the eyes; have or use the sense of sight [We *saw* two birds. I don't *see* so well.] **2** to get the meaning of; understand [Do you *see* the point of the joke?] **3** to visit with [We stopped to *see* a friend.] **4** to go to for information or advice; consult [*See* a doctor about your cough.] **5** to think or try to remember [Let me *see*, where did I put that?] —**saw, seen, see′ing**

seek (sēk) *v.* to try to find; search for [to *seek* gold]. —**sought, seek′ing**

seen (sēn) *past participle of* **see.**

sel·fish (sel′fish) *adj.* caring too much about oneself, with little or no thought or care for others. —**self′ish·ly** *adv.* — **self′ish·ness** *n.*

send (send) *v.* **1** to cause to be carried [Food was *sent* by plane.] **2** to cause a message to be transmitted by mail, radio, or other means [I will *send* the letter tomorrow.] **3** to cause or force to go [The teacher *sent* her home.] —**sent, send′ing**

a	ask, fat
ā	ape, date
ä	car, lot
e	elf, ten
ē	even, meet
i	is, hit
ī	ice, fire
ō	open, go
ô	law, horn
oi	oil, point
oo	look, pull
oo	ooze, tool
ou	out, crowd
u	up, cut
ʉ	fur, fern
ə	a in ago
	e in agent
	e in father
	i in unity
	o in collect
	u in focus
ch	chin, arch
ŋ	ring, singer
sh	she, dash
th	thin, truth
th	then, father
zh	s in pleasure

sent (sent) *past tense and past participle of* **send**.

serve (surv) *v.* **1** to aid; to help [She *served* her country well.] **2** to wait on [The waiter *served* our table first.] —**served, serv′ing**

set (set) *v.* **1** to put in a certain place or position [*Set* the book on the table.] **2** to put in order or in the right condition, position, etc.; arrange; adjust [to *set* a trap; to *set* a thermostat; to *set* a broken bone; to *set* a table for a meal.] **3** to establish or fix, as a time for a meeting, a price, a rule, a limit, etc. **4** to sink below the horizon [The sun *sets* in the west.] —**set, set′ting** ◆*n.* **1** a number of parts put together, as in a cabinet [a TV *set*]. **2** in mathematics, any collection of units, points, numbers, etc.

set·ting (set′iŋ) *n.* the time, place, and circumstances of an event, story, play, etc.

shad·ow (shad′ō) *n.* the darkness or the dark shape cast upon a surface by something cutting off light from it [Her large hat put her face in *shadow*. His hand cast a *shadow* on the wall.]

shadow

shape (shāp) *n.* the way a thing looks because of its outline; outer form; figure [The cloud had the *shape* of a lamb.] ◆*v.* to give a certain shape to; form [The potter *shaped* the clay into a bowl.] —**shaped, shap′ing**

share (sher) *n.* a part that each one of a group gets or has [your *share* of the cake; my *share* of the blame]. ◆*v.* to have a share of with others; have or use together [The three of you will *share* the back seat.] —**shared, shar′ing**

sharp (shärp) *adj.* **1** having a thin edge for cutting or a fine point for piercing [a *sharp* knife; a *sharp* needle]. **2** very clever or shrewd [a *sharp* mind]. ◆*adv.* exactly or promptly [She gets up at 6:30 *sharp*.] —**sharp′ly** *adv.* —**sharp′ness** *n.*

sheep (shēp) *n.* an animal that chews its cud and is related to the goat. Its body is covered with heavy wool, and its flesh is used as food, called mutton. —*pl.* **sheep**

shelf (shelf) *n.* a thin, flat length of wood, metal, etc., fastened against a wall or built into a frame so as to hold things [the top *shelf* of a bookcase]. —*pl.* **shelves**

shelves (shelvz) *n. plural of* **shelf**.

shine (shīn) *v.* **1** to give off light or reflect light; be bright [The sun *shines*. Her hair *shone*.] **2** to make bright by polishing [to *shine* shoes]. —**shone** or **shined, shin′ing** ◆*n.* the act of polishing, as shoes.

shirt (shurt) *n.* **1** the common garment worn by a boy or man on the upper part of the body.

shi·ver (shiv′ər) *v.* to shake or tremble, often from fear or cold [We *shivered* when we heard scary sounds.]

shoot (shoot) *v.* to send a bullet, arrow, etc., from [to *shoot* a gun]. —**shot, shoot′ing** ◆*n.* a new growth; sprout. —**shoot′er** *n.*

short (shôrt) *adj.* **1** not measuring much from end to end or from beginning to end; not long [a *short* stick; a *short* trip; a *short* novel; a *short* wait]. **2** not tall; low [a *short* tree]. **3** less or having less than what is enough or correct [Our supply of food is *short*. We are *short* ten dollars.] **4** taking a shorter time to say than other sounds [The "e" in "bed" and the "i" in "rib" are *short*.] ◆*adv.* so as to be short [Cut your speech *short*. We fell *short* of our goal.] ◆*v.* to give less than what is needed, usual, etc. [The cashier *shorted* the customer a dollar.]

shoul·der (shōl′dər) *n.* the part of the body to which an arm or foreleg is connected.

should·n't (shŏŏd′nt) should not.

shov·el (shuv′əl) *n.* a tool with a broad scoop and a handle, for lifting and moving loose material. ◆*v.* to lift and move with a shovel [to *shovel* coal]. —**shov′eled** or **shov′elled, shov′el·ing** or **shov′el·ling**

shy (shī) *adj.* 1 easily frightened; timid [a *shy* animal]. 2 not at ease with other people; bashful [a *shy* child]. —**shi′er** or **shy′er, shi′est** or **shy′est** —**shy′ly** *adv.* —**shy′ness** *n.*

side·walk (sīd′wôk) *n.* a path for walking; usually paved, along the side of a street.

sigh (sī) *v.* to let out a long, deep, sounded breath, usually to show that one is sad, tired, relieved, etc. ◆*n.* the act or sound of sighing [She breathed a *sigh* of relief.]

sight (sīt) *n.* 1 something that is seen; especially, something unusual worth seeing [The Grand Canyon is a *sight* you won't forget.] 2 the ability to see; vision; eyesight [He lost his *sight* in the war.] 3 the distance over which one can see [The airplane passed out of *sight*.] ◆*v.* to see [The sailor *sighted* land.]

sign (sīn) *n.* 1 a thing or act that stands for something else; symbol [Black is worn as a *sign* of grief. She saluted the flag as a *sign* of respect. The *sign* (+) means "add."] 2 a board, card, etc., put up in a public place, with information, a warning, etc., on it [The *sign* said, "Do not enter."] 3 anything that tells of the existence or coming of something else [Red spots on the face may be a *sign* of measles.] ◆*v.* to write one's name on [to *sign* a contract to make it legal].

since (sins) *adv.* from then until now [Lynn came Monday and has been here ever *since*.] ◆*prep.* from or during the time given until now [I've been up *since* dawn.] ◆*conj.* 1 after the time that [It's been two years *since* I saw you.] 2 because [You may have these tools, *since* I no longer need them.]

sis·ter (sis′tər) *n.* a girl or woman as she is related to the other children of her parents.

sixth (siksth) *adj.* coming after five others; 6th in order. ◆*n.* one of the six equal parts of something; 1/6.

six·ty (siks′tē) *n.* the cardinal number that is equal to six times ten; 60. —*pl.* **six′ties**

size (sīz) *n.* 1 the amount of space taken up by a thing; how large or how small a thing is [Tell me the *size* of your room. He is strong for his *size*.] 2 any of a series of measures, often numbered, for grading things [She wears a *size* 12 dress. These are jumbo *size* peanuts.] ◆*v.* to arrange according to size. —**sized, siz′ing**

slight (slīt) *adj.* small in amount or degree; not great, strong, important, etc. [a *slight* change in temperature; a *slight* advantage; a *slight* bruise]. —**slight′ly** *adv.*

slip (slip) *v.* 1 to go or pass quietly or without being noticed; escape [We *slipped* out the door. It *slipped* my mind. Time *slipped* by.] 2 to move, shift, or drop, as by accident [The plate *slipped* from my hand.] 3 to slide by accident [He *slipped* on the ice.] —**slipped, slip′ping**

slum·ber (slum′bər) *v.* 1 to sleep. 2 to be quiet or inactive [The volcano has *slumbered* for years.] ◆*n.* sleep.

sly (slī) *adj.* able to fool or trick others; cunning; crafty [the *sly* fox]. —**sli′er** or **sly′er, sli′est** or **sly′est** —**sly′ly** or **sli′ly** *adv.*

shovel

a	ask, fat
ā	ape, date
ä	car, lot
e	elf, ten
ē	even, meet
i	is, hit
ī	ice, fire
ō	open, go
ô	law, horn
oi	oil, point
ŏŏ	look, pull
ōō	ooze, tool
ou	out, crowd
u	up, cut
ʉ	fur, fern
ə	a in ago
	e in agent
	e in father
	i in unity
	o in collect
	u in focus
ch	chin, arch
ŋ	ring, singer
sh	she, dash
th	thin, truth
th	then, father
zh	s in pleasure

smart (smärt) *adj.* **1** intelligent or clever [a *smart* student]. **2** neat, clean, and well-groomed. **3** of the newest fashion; stylish [a *smart* new hat]. ◆*v.* to cause a sharp, stinging pain [A bee sting *smarts*.] —**smart′ly** *adv.* —**smart′ness** *n.*

smile (smīl) *v.* to show that one is pleased, happy, amused, etc., or sarcastic or scornful, by making the corners of the mouth turn up. —**smiled, smil′ing** ◆*n.* the act of smiling or the look on one's face when one smiles.

smog·gy (smôg′ē *or* smäg′ē) *adj.* full of polluted air. —**smog′gi· er, smog′gi·est**

soak (sōk) *v.* **1** to make or become completely wet by keeping or staying in a liquid [She *soaked* her sore hand in hot water. Let the beans *soak* overnight to soften them.] **2** to suck up or absorb [Use a sponge to *soak* up that water.] ◆*n.* the act of soaking.

some (sum) *adj.* **1** being a certain one or ones not named or not known [*Some* people were playing ball.] **2** being of a certain but not a definite number or amount [Have *some* candy.] ◆*pron.* a certain number or amount, but not all [Take *some*.]

somewhat (sum′hwut *or* sum′wut) *adv.* to some degree; rather; a little [They are *somewhat* late.]

soon (sōōn) *adv.* **1** in a short time; before much time has passed [Spring will *soon* be here.] **2** fast or quickly [as *soon* as possible]. **3** ahead of time; early [She left too *soon*.] —**soon′er, soon′est**

soot (soot) *n.* a black powder formed when some things burn. It is mostly carbon and makes smoke gray or black.

soothe (sōō*th*) *v.* **1** to make quiet or calm by being gentle or friendly [The clerk *soothed* the angry customer with helpful answers.] **2** to take away some of the pain or sorrow of; ease [I hope this lotion will *soothe* your sunburn.] —**soothed, sooth′ing** —**sooth′ing·ly** *adv.*

sought (sôt *or* sät) *past tense and past participle of* **seek**.

spare (sper) *v.* to save or free from something [*Spare* us from listening to that story again.] ◆ *adj.* kept for use when needed [a *spare* tire].

speak (spēk) *v.* **1** to say something with the voice; talk [They *spoke* to each other on the phone.] **2** to make a speech [Who *speaks* first on the show?]

spe·cial (spesh′əl) *adj.* **1** not like others; different; distinctive [The cook has a *special* recipe for tacos.] **2** unusual; extraordinary [Your idea has *special* merit.] **3** more than others; chief; main [her *special* friend]. —**spe′cial·ly** *adv.*

spend (spend) *v.* to pay out or give up, as money, time, or effort [He *spent* $50 for food. *Spend* some time with me.] —**spent, spend′ing** —**spend′er** *n.*

spic·y (spī′sē) *adj.* seasoned with spice or spices. —**spic′i·er, spic′i·est**

spied (spīd) *past tense and past participle of* **spy**.

spill (spil) *v.* to let flow over or run out [Who *spilled* water on the floor? Try not to *spill* any sugar.] —**spilled** or **spilt, spill′ing** ◆*n.* **1** the act of spilling. **2** a fall or tumble, as from a horse: *used only in everyday talk.*

splash (splash) *v.* **1** to make a liquid scatter and fall in drops [to *splash* water or mud about]. **2** to dash a liquid on, so as to wet or soil [The car *splashed* my coat.] —**splash′y** *adj.*

split (split) **v.** to separate or divide along the length into two or more parts [to *split* a wiener bun]. —**split, split′ting ◆ n.** a break, crack, or tear [a *split* in the seam of a dress]. ◆ **adj.** broken into parts; divided.

spoil (spoil) **v.** **1** to make or become useless, worthless, or rotten; to damage; to ruin [Ink stains *spoiled* the paper.] **2** to cause a person to ask for or expect too much by giving in to all of that person's wishes [to *spoil* a child]. —**spoiled** or **spoilt, spoil′ing**

sprang (spraŋ) *past tense of* **spring**.

spray (sprā) **n.** a mist of tiny drops, as of water thrown off from a waterfall. ◆ **v.** to put something on in a spray [to *spray* a car with paint]. —**spray′er n.**

spread (spred) **v.** **1** to open out or stretch out, in space or time [*Spread* out the tablecloth. The eagle *spread* its wings. Our trip *spread* out over two weeks.] **2** to put or cover in a thin layer [to *spread* bread with jelly]. ◆ **n.** **1** a cloth cover, as for a table or bed. **2** any soft substance, as jam or butter, that can be spread in a layer. —**spread′er n.**

spring (spriŋ) **v.** **1** to move suddenly and quickly; leap; jump up [I *sprang* to my feet.] **2** to snap back into position or shape, as a rubber band that is stretched and then let go. —**sprang** or **sprung, sprung, spring′ing** ◆ **n.** **1** a device, as a coil of wire, that returns to its original shape when pressure on it is released. Springs are used in beds and automobiles to take up shock or in clocks, etc., to make them go. **2** water flowing up from the ground. **3** the season when plants begin to grow, between winter and summer.

spy (spī) **n.** a person who watches others secretly and carefully. —*pl.* **spies ◆ v.** to watch closely and secretly [She likes to *spy* on her neighbors.] —**spied, spy′ing**

squirm (skwʉrm) **v.** to twist and turn the body as a snake does; wriggle; writhe [The rabbit *squirmed* out of the trap.]

stain (stān) **v.** to spoil with dirt or a patch of color; to soil or spot [The rug was *stained* with ink.] ◆ **n.** a dirty or colored spot [grass *stains*].

stand (stand) **v.** **1** to be or get in an upright position on one's feet [*Stand* by your desk.] **2** to be or place in an upright position on its base, bottom, etc. [Our trophy *stands* on the shelf. *Stand* the broom in the corner.] **3** to be placed or situated [Our house *stands* on a hill.] —**stood, stand′ing**

start (stärt) **v.** **1** to begin to go, do, act, be, etc. [We *start* for Toledo today. The show *starts* at 8:30.] **2** to cause to begin; set in motion or action [*Start* the car. Who *started* the fight?] ◆ **n.** the act of starting or beginning.

stead·y (sted′ē) **adj.** **1** firm or stable; not shaky [a *steady* chair]. **2** not changing or letting up; regular [a *steady* rain]. —**stead′i·er, stead′i·est**

steel (stēl) **n.** a hard, tough metal made of iron mixed with a little carbon.

stem (stem) **n.** the main part of a plant or tree that grows up from the ground and bears the leaves, flowers, or fruit.

step (step) **n.** **1** the act of moving and placing the foot forward, backward, sideways, up, or down, as in walking, dancing, or climbing. **2** a place to rest the foot in going up or down, as a stair or the rung of a ladder. ◆ **v.** to move by taking a step or steps. —**stepped, step′ping**

a	ask, fat
ā	ape, date
ä	car, lot
e	elf, ten
ē	even, meet
i	is, hit
ī	ice, fire
ō	open, go
ô	law, horn
oi	oil, point
ꝏ	look, pull
o͞o	ooze, tool
ou	out, crowd
u	up, cut
ʉ	fur, fern
ə	a in ago
	e in agent
	e in father
	i in unity
	o in collect
	u in focus
ch	chin, arch
ŋ	ring, singer
sh	she, dash
th	thin, truth
th	then, father
zh	s in pleasure

sting (stiŋ) *v.* **1** to hurt by pricking [Wasps can *sting* you.] **2** to cause or feel sharp pain [The cold wind *stung* her cheeks.] —**stung, sting′ing** ◆*n.* the act or power of stinging [The *sting* of a bee may be dangerous.]

stir (stʉr) *v.* to move or shake slightly [Not a leaf *stirred* in the quiet air.] —**stirred, stir′ring**

stone (stōn) *n.* **1** hard mineral matter that is found in the earth but is not metal; rock [a monument built of *stone*]. **2** a small piece of this [Don't throw *stones*. Rubies are precious *stones*.]

stood (stood) *past tense and past participle of* **stand.**

stop (stäp) *v.* **1** to halt or keep from going on, moving, acting, etc.; bring or come to an end [My watch *stopped*. The noise *stopped*. *Stop* the car. They *stopped* us from talking.] **2** to clog or block [The drain in the sink is *stopped* up.] **3** to stay or visit [We *stopped* there overnight.] —**stopped, stop′ping** ◆*n.* **1** a place stopped at [a *stop* on a bus route]. **2** the act or fact of stopping; finish; end [Put a *stop* to this argument.]

stran·ger (strān′jər) *n.* **1** a person who is new to a place; outsider or foreigner. **2** a person not known to one [Don't speak to *strangers*.]

straw·ber·ry (strô′ber′ē) *n.* the small, red, juicy fruit of a low plant of the rose family. —*pl.* **straw′ber′ries**

stream (strēm) *n.* a flow of water; especially, a small river. ◆*v.* **1** to flow in a stream. **2** to pour out or flow [eyes *streaming* with tears].

street (strēt) *n.* a road in a city or town; also, such a road with its sidewalks and buildings.

strike (strīk) *v.* **1** to hit by giving a blow, coming against with force, etc. [Nina *struck* him in anger. The car *struck* the curb.] **2** to make a sound by hitting some part [The clock *struck* one. *Strike* middle C on the piano.] **3** to set on fire as by rubbing [to *strike* a match]. **4** to stop working until certain demands have been met [The workers are *striking* for shorter hours.] —**struck, struck** or **strick′en, strik′ing**

string (striŋ) *n.* **1** a thick thread or thin strip of cloth, leather, etc., used for tying or pulling; cord. **2** a number of things in a row [a *string* of lights]. ◆*v.* **1** to put on a string [to *string* beads]. **2** to stretch like a string; extend [to *string* telephone wires on poles; to *string* out a speech]. —**strung, string′ing**

strong (strôŋ) *adj.* **1** having great force or power; not weak; powerful [a *strong* person; *strong* winds]. **2** having a powerful effect on the senses or mind; not mild [a *strong* taste, smell, light, sound, liking, etc.] —**strong′ly** *adv.* —**strong′ness** *n.*

struck (struk) *past tense and a past participle of* **strike.**

stud·y (stud′ē) *v.* **1** to try to learn by reading, thinking, etc. [to *study* law]. **2** to look at or into carefully; examine or investigate [We must *study* the problem of crime.] **3** to read so as to understand and remember [to *study* a lesson]. —**stud′ied, stud′y·ing** ◆*n.* **1** a branch of learning; subject [the *study* of medicine]. **2** a room used for studying, reading, etc. —*pl.* **stud′ies**

sug·ar (shoog′ər) *n.* any of certain sweet substances in the form of crystals that dissolve in water. Glucose, lactose, and sucrose are different kinds of sugar. Sucrose is the common sugar used to sweeten food.

sweat·er (swet′ər) *n.* a knitted outer garment for the upper part of the body.

swim (swim) *v.* to move in water by working the arms, legs, fins, etc. —**swam, swum, swim′ming** ◆*n.* an act, time, or distance of swimming. —**swim′mer** *n.*

take (tāk) *v.* **1** to get hold of; grasp [*Take* my hand as we cross the street.] **2** to write down; copy [*Take* notes on the lecture.] **3** to carry [*Take* your skis with you.] **4** to lead or bring [I *took* Lee to the movie. This road *takes* us to the park.] —**took, tak′en, tak′ing**

tax (taks) *n.* money that one must pay to help support a government. It is usually a percentage of one's income or of the value of something bought or owned. —*pl.* **tax′es** —**tax′a·ble** *adj.*

teach·er (tēch′ər) *n.* a person who teaches, especially in a school or college.

team (tēm) *n.* **1** two or more horses, oxen, etc., harnessed together as for pulling a plow or wagon. **2** a group of people working together or playing together in a contest against another such group [a *team* of scientists; a baseball *team*]. ◆*v.* to join together in a team [Let's *team* up with them.]

teeth (tēth) *n. plural of* **tooth**.

ten·der (ten′dər) *adj.* **1** soft or delicate and easily chewed or cut [a *tender* piece of meat]. **2** feeling pain or hurting easily; sensitive [My sprained ankle still feels *tender.*] **3** warm and gentle; loving [a *tender* smile].

Tex·as (teks′əs) a state in the south central part of the U.S.: abbreviated **Tex., TX** —**Tex′an** *adj., n.*

than (*than or* thən) *conj.* compared to. *Than* is used before the second part of a comparison [I am taller *than* you.]

thank (thaŋk) *v.* to say that one is grateful to another for a kindness [We *thanked* her for her help.]

that (*that or* thət) *pron.* **1** the person or thing mentioned [*That* is José.] **2** who, whom, or which [She's the one *that* I saw. Here's the book *that* I borrowed.] —*pl.* **those**

that's (*thats or* thəts) that is.

thaw (thô) *v.* **1** to melt [The snow *thawed.*] **2** to become unfrozen: said of frozen foods. ◆*n.* weather that is warm enough to melt snow and ice.

them (them) *pron.* the form of **they** that is used as the object of a verb or preposition [I met *them* at the airport. Give the flowers to *them.*]

there's (therz) there is.

they'll (thāl) **1** they will. **2** they shall.

they're (ther) they are.

thief (thēf) *n.* a person who steals, especially one who steals secretly. —*pl.* **thieves** (thēvz)

think (thiŋk) *v.* **1** to use the mind; reason [*Think* before you act.] **2** to form or have in the mind [She was *thinking* happy thoughts.] —**thought, think′ing**

third (thurd) *adj.* coming after two others; 3rd in order. ◆*n.* one of three equal parts of something; 1/3.

thir·teen (thur′tēn′) *n., adj.* three more than ten; the number 13.

thir·ty (thurt′ē) *n., adj.* three times ten; the number 30. —*pl.* **thir′ties**

thought[1] (thôt) *n.* **1** the act or process of thinking [When deep in *thought*, he doesn't hear.] **2** what one thinks; idea, opinion, plan, etc. [a penny for your *thoughts*].

thread

a	ask, fat
ā	ape, date
ä	car, lot
e	elf, ten
ē	even, meet
i	is, hit
ī	ice, fire
ō	open, go
ô	law, horn
oi	oil, point
σο	look, pull
ōō	ooze, tool
ou	out, crowd
u	up, cut
u	fur, fern
ə	a in ago
	e in agent
	e in father
	i in unity
	o in collect
	u in focus
ch	chin, arch
ŋ	ring, singer
sh	she, dash
th	thin, truth
th	then, father
zh	s in pleasure

187

thought² (thôt) *past tense and past participle of* **think.**

thread (thred) *n.* a very thin cord used in sewing and made of strands of spun cotton, silk, etc., twisted together. ◆*v.* to put a thread through the eye of [to *thread* a needle]. —**thread′like** *adj.*

thrill (thril) *v.* to feel or make greatly excited; shiver or tingle with strong feeling [She *thrilled* at the praise. That movie *thrilled* us.] ◆*n.* a strong feeling of excitement that makes one shiver [Seeing a lion gave me a *thrill.*]

throat (thrōt) *n.* 1 the front part of the neck. 2 the upper part of the passage from the mouth to the stomach or lungs [I have a sore *throat.*]

throne (thrōn) *n.* the raised chair on which a king or other important person sits during ceremonies.

through (thrōō) *prep.* 1 in one side and out the other side of; from end to end of [The nail went *through* the board. We drove *through* the tunnel.] 2 from the beginning to the end of [We stayed in Maine *through* the summer.] ◆*adv.* in a complete and thorough way; entirely [We were soaked *through* by the rain.] ◆*adj.* finished [Are you *through* with your homework?]

throw (thrō) *v.* to send through the air by a fast motion of the arm; hurl, toss, etc. [to *throw* a ball]. —**threw, thrown, throw′ing** ◆*n.* the act of throwing [The fast *throw* put the runner out at first base.]

thumb (thum) *n.* the short, thick finger nearest the wrist. ◆*v.* to handle, turn, soil, etc., with the thumb [to *thumb* the pages of a book].

tide (tīd) *n.* the regular rise and fall of the ocean's surface, about every twelve hours, caused by the attraction of the moon and sun.

toy

◆*v.* to help in overcoming a time of trouble [Will ten dollars *tide* you over till Monday?] —**tid′ed, tid′ing**

tie (tī) *v.* 1 to bind together or fasten with string, rope, cord, etc. [They *tied* his hands together. *Tie* the boat to the pier.] 2 to equal, as in a score [Pablo *tied* with Carmela for first place.] —**tied, ty′ing** ◆*n.* 1 a shorter word for **necktie.** 2 the fact of being equal, as in a score; also, a contest in which scores are equal. —*pl.* **ties**

to (tōō *or* too *or* tə) *prep.* 1 in the direction of [Turn *to* the right.] 2 on, onto, against, etc. [Put your hand *to* your mouth. Apply the lotion *to* the skin.]

too (tōō) *adv.* 1 in addition; besides; also [You come, *too.*] 2 more than enough [This hat is *too* big.] 3 very [You are *too* kind.]

toss (tôs *or* täs) *v.* to throw from the hand in a light way [to *toss* a ball]

tough (tuf) *adj.* 1 able to bend or twist without tearing or breaking [*tough* rubber]. 2 rough or brutal [Don't get *tough* with me.]

town (toun) *n.* a place where there are a large number of houses and other buildings, larger than a village but smaller than a city.

toy (toi) *n.* a thing to play with; especially, a plaything for children. ◆*adj.* 1 like a toy in size or use [a *toy* dog]. 2 made for use as a toy; especially, made as a small model [a *toy* train].

track (trak) *n.* 1 a mark left in passing, as a footprint or wheel rut. 2 a path or trail. ◆*v.* 1 to follow the tracks of [We *tracked* the fox to its den.] 2 to make tracks or dirty marks [The children *tracked* up the clean floor.]

treas·ure (trezh′ər) *n.* money or jewels collected and stored up.

trip (trip) *v.* to stumble or make stumble [She *tripped* over the rug. Bill put out his foot and *tripped* me.] —**tripped, trip′ping** ◆*n.* a traveling from one place to another and returning; journey, especially a short one.

tur·key (tʉr′kē) *n.* ☆**1** a large, wild or tame bird, originally of North America, with a small head and spreading tail. ☆**2** its flesh, used as food. —*pl.* **tur′keys** or **tur′key**

twen·ty (twen′tē) *n., adj.* two times ten; the number 20 —*pl.* **twen′ties**

two (to͞o) *n., adj.* one more than one; the number 2. —**in two,** in two parts.

un- **1** *a prefix meaning* not *or* the opposite of [An *unhappy* person is one who is not happy, but sad.] **2** *a prefix meaning* to reverse *or* undo the action of [To *untie* a shoelace is to reverse the action of tying it.]

un·a·ble (un ā′bəl) *adj.* not able; not having the means or power to do something.

un·but·ton (un but′n) *v.* to unfasten the button or buttons of.

un·clean (un klēn′) *adj.* dirty; filthy.

un·der (un′dər) *prep.* in or to a place, position, amount, value, etc., lower than; below [He sang *under* her window. It rolled *under* the table. It weighs *under* a pound.] ◆*adv.* less in amount, value, etc. [It cost two dollars or *under*.]

un·eas·y (un ē′zē) *adj.* **1** having or giving no ease; not comfortable [an *uneasy* conscience]. **2** worried; anxious [Dad felt *uneasy* when I was late.] —**un·eas′i·er, un·eas′i·est**

un·e·ven (un ē′vən) *adj.* not even, level, or smooth; irregular [*uneven* ground]. —**un·e′ven·ly adv.** —**un·e′ven·ness n.**

un·load (un lōd′) *v.* to take a load or cargo from a truck, ship, etc.

un·luck·y (un luk′ē) *adj.* having or bringing bad luck; not lucky; unfortunate [There is a superstition that breaking a mirror is *unlucky*.] —**un·luck′i·er, un·luck′i·est** —**un·luck′i·ly adv.**

un·paid (un pād′) *adj.* not receiving pay [an *unpaid* helper].

un·pre·pared (un′prē perd′) *adj.* not prepared or ready [We are still *unprepared* for the visitors.]

un·true (un tro͞o′) *adj.* **1** not correct; false. **2** not faithful or loyal. —**un·tru′ly adv.**

u·su·al (yo͞o′zho͞o əl) *adj.* such as is most often seen, heard, or used; common; normal [the *usual* time].—**u′su·al·ly adv.**

un·wrap (un rap′) *v.* to open by taking off the wrapping; also, to become opened in this way. —**un·wrapped′, un·wrap′ping**

use (yo͞oz) *v.* **1** to put or bring into service or action [*Use* the vacuum cleaner on the rugs. What kind of toothpaste do you *use*?] **2** to do away with by using; consume [She *used* up all the soap. Don't *use* up your energy.] —**used, us′ing**

used (yo͞ozd) *adj.* that has been used; not new; secondhand [*used* cars].

ver·y (ver′ē) *adv.* in a high degree; to a great extent; extremely [*very* cold; *very* funny; *very* sad].

a	ask, fat
ā	ape, date
ä	car, lot
e	elf, ten
ē	even, meet
i	is, hit
ī	ice, fire
ō	open, go
ô	law, horn
oi	oil, point
o͝o	look, pull
o͞o	ooze, tool
ou	out, crowd
u	up, cut
ʉ	fur, fern
ə	a in ago
	e in agent
	e in father
	i in unity
	o in collect
	u in focus
ch	chin, arch
ŋ	ring, singer
sh	she, dash
th	thin, truth
th	then, father
zh	s in pleasure

wagon

wag·on (wag′ən) *n.* a vehicle with four wheels, especially for carrying heavy loads.

wal·let (wôl′ət *or* wäl′ət) *n.* ☆a thin, flat case for carrying money, cards, etc., in the pocket.

was (wuz *or* wäz) *the form of* **be** *showing the past time with singular nouns and with* I, he, she, *or* it.

was·n't (wuz′ənt *or* wäz′ənt) was not.

watch (wäch *or* wôch) *v.* **1** to keep one's sight on; look at [We *watched* the parade.] **2** to take care of; look after; guard [The shepherd *watched* his flock.] ◆*n.* **1** the act of watching or guarding [The dog keeps *watch* over the house.] **2** a device for telling time that is like a clock but small enough to be worn, as on the wrist, or carried in the pocket. — *pl.* **watch′es**

wa·ter (wôt′ər) *n.* the colorless liquid that falls as rain, is found in springs, rivers, lakes, and oceans, and forms a large part of the cells of all living things. It is made up of hydrogen and oxygen, with the chemical formula H_2O. ◆*v.* **1** to give water to [to *water* a horse]. **2** to supply with water, as by sprinkling [to *water* a lawn].

wax (waks) *n.* **1** a yellow substance that bees make and use for building honeycombs; beeswax. **2** any substance like this, as paraffin. Wax is used to make candles, polishes, etc. ◆*v.* to put wax or polish on.

weak (wēk) *adj.* having little strength, force, or power; not strong or firm [*weak* from illness].

wear (wer) *v.* **1** to have or carry on the body [*Wear* your coat. Do you *wear* glasses?] **2** to have or show in the way one appears [She

whale

wore a frown. He *wears* his hair long.] **3** to make or become damaged, used up, etc. by use or friction [She *wore* her jeans to rags. The water is *wearing* away the river bank.] —**wore, worn, wear′ing**

weight (wāt) *n.* **1** heaviness, the quality a thing has because of the pull of gravity on it. **2** amount of heaviness [What is your *weight*?] **3** any solid mass used for its heaviness [to lift *weights* for exercise; a paper*weight*.]

we'll (wēl) **1** we shall. **2** we will.

wet (wet) *adj.* covered or soaked with water or some other liquid [Wipe it off with a *wet* rag.] —**wet′ter, wet′test**

whack (hwak) *v.* to hit or slap with a sharp sound. ◆*n.* a blow that makes a sharp sound; also, this sound.

whale (hwāl) *n.* a very large mammal that lives in the sea and looks like a fish.

wheel (hwēl) *n.* a round disk or frame that turns on an axle fixed at its center [a wagon *wheel*]. ◆*v.* to move on wheels or in a vehicle with wheels [to *wheel* a grocery cart].

where's (hwerz *or* werz) **1** where is. **2** where has.

wheth·er (hwe*th*′ər) *conj.* **1** if it is true or likely that [I don't know *whether* I can go.] **2** in either case that [It makes no difference *whether* he comes or not.]

which (hwich) *pron.* what one or what ones of those being talked about or suggested [*Which* will you choose?]

while (hwīl) *n.* a period of time [I waited a short *while*.] ◆*conj.* during the time that [I read a book *while* I waited.]

whine (hwīn *or* wīn) *v.* to make a long, high sound or cry [The injured dog *whined*.] —**whined, whin′ing**

190

whirl (hwʉrl *or* wʉrl) *v.* to turn rapidly around and around; spin fast [The dancers *whirled* around the room.]

whisk (hwisk) *v.* to move, brush, etc., with a quick, sweeping motion [He *whisked* the lint from his coat with a brush.] ◆*n.* **1** a small broom with a short handle, for brushing clothes: *the full name is* **whisk broom**. **2** a kitchen tool made up of wire loops fixed in a handle, for whipping eggs, etc.

whisper (hwis′pər) *v.* to speak or say in a low, soft voice, especially without vibrating the vocal cords. ◆*n.* soft, low tone of voice [to speak in a *whisper*].

who (hoo) *pron.* what person or persons? [*Who* helped you?]

whole (hōl) *adj.* **1** not divided or cut up; in one piece [Put *whole* carrots in the stew.] **2** having all its parts, complete [The *whole* opera is on two records.] ◆*n.* the total amount [He saved the *whole* of his allowance.] —**whole′ness** *n.*

wife (wīf) *n.* the woman to whom a man is married; married woman. —*pl.* **wives**

win·ner (win′ər) *n.* **1** one that wins. **2** a person who seems very likely to win or be successful: *used only in everyday talk.*

witch (wich) *n.* a person, now especially a woman, who is believed to have magic power with the help of the devil. —*pl.* **witch′es**

wives (wīvz) *n.* *plural of* **wife**.

wolf (woolf) *n.* **1** a wild animal that looks like a dog. It kills other animals for food. **2** a person who is fierce, cruel, greedy, etc. —*pl.* **wolves**

wolves (woolvz) *n.* *plural of* **wolf**.

wom·an (woom′ən) *n.* **1** an adult, female human being. **2** women as a group —*pl.* **wom′en**

wom·en (wim′ən) *n.* *plural of* **woman**.

won′t (wōnt) will not.

wood·en (wood′n) *adj.* made of wood.

wool (wool) *n.* **1** the soft, curly hair of sheep or the hair of some other animals, as the goat or llama. **2** yarn, cloth, or clothing made from such hair.

wore (wôr) *past tense of* **wear**.

work·book (wʉrk′book) *n.* ☆a book that has questions and exercises to be worked out by students.

wor·ry (wʉr′ē) *v.* to be or make troubled in mind; feel or make uneasy or anxious [Don't *worry*. Her absence *worried* us.] —**wor′ried, wor′ry·ing** ◆*n.* a troubled feeling; anxiety; care [sick with *worry*]. —*pl.* **wor′ries**

would (wood) *the past tense of* **will** [He promised that he *would* return.]

would·n′t (wood′nt) would not.

would′ve (wood′uv) would have.

wrap (rap) *v.* **1** to wind or fold around something [She *wrapped* a scarf around her head.] **2** to cover in this way [They *wrapped* the baby in a blanket.] **3** to cover with paper, etc. [to *wrap* a present]. —**wrapped** or **wrapt** (rapt), **wrap′ping** ◆*n.* an outer covering or outer garment [Put your *wraps* in the closet.]

wreck (rek) *n.* the remains of something that has been destroyed or badly damaged [an old *wreck* stranded on the reef]. ◆*v.* to destroy or damage badly; ruin [to *wreck* a car in an accident; to *wreck* one's plans for a picnic].

wren (ren) *n.* a small songbird with a long bill and a stubby tail that tilts up.

wrin·kle (riŋ′kəl) *n.* a small or uneven crease or fold [*wrinkles* in a coat]. ◆*v.* **1** to make wrinkles in [a brow that is *wrinkled* with care]. **2** to form wrinkles [This cloth *wrinkles* easily.] — **wrin′kled, wrin′kling**

wolf

a	ask, fat
ā	ape, date
ä	car, lot
e	elf, ten
ē	even, meet
i	is, hit
ī	ice, fire
ō	open, go
ô	law, horn
oi	oil, point
oo	look, pull
ōo	ooze, tool
ou	out, crowd
u	up, cut
ʉ	fur, fern
ə	a in ago
	e in agent
	e in father
	i in unity
	o in collect
	u in focus
ch	chin, arch
ŋ	ring, singer
sh	she, dash
th	thin, truth
th	then, father
zh	s in pleasure

write (rīt) **v.** **1** to form words, letters, etc., as with a pen or pencil. **2** to form the words, letters, etc., of [*Write* your address here.] **3** to be the author or composer of [Dickens *wrote* novels. Mozart *wrote* symphonies.] **4** to fill in or cover with writing [to *write* a check; to *write* ten pages]. **5** to send a message in writing; write a letter [*Write* me every week. He *wrote* that he was ill.]—**wrote, writ′ten, writ′ing**

writ·er (rīt′ər) **n.** a person who writes, especially one whose work is writing books, essays, articles, etc.; author.

wrong (rôŋ) **adj.** **1** not right, just, or good; unlawful, wicked, or bad [It is *wrong* to steal.] **2** not the one that is true, correct, wanted, etc. [the *wrong* answer]. **3** in error; mistaken [He's not *wrong*.] ◆**n.** something wrong; especially, a wicked or unjust act [Does she know right from *wrong*?] ◆**adv.** in a wrong way, direction, etc.; incorrectly [You did it *wrong*.] —**wrong′ly adv.** —**wrong′ness n.**

wrote (rōt) *past tense of* **write.**

year (yir) **n.** **1** a period of 365 days, or, in leap year, 366, divided into 12 months and beginning January 1. It is based on the time taken by the earth to go completely around the sun, about 365 1/4 days. **2** any period of twelve months starting at any time [She was six *years* old in July.]

yell (yel) **v.** to cry out loudly; scream. ◆**n.** **1** a loud shout. **2** a cheer by a crowd, usually in rhythm, as at a football game.

your (yoor) **pron.** of you or done by you. *This possessive form of* **you** *is used before a noun and thought of as an adjective* [*your* book; *your* work]. *See also* **yours**.

you're (yoor *or* yoor) you are.

yours (yoorz) **pron.** the one or the ones that belong to you. *This form of* **your** *is used when it is not followed by a noun* [Is this pen *yours*? *Yours* cost more than ours.] *Yours is used as a polite closing of a letter, often with truly, sincerely, etc.*

you've (yoov) you have.